MznLnx

Missing Links Exam Preps

Exam Prep for

Financial Markets & Institutions

Saunders & Cornett, 3rd Edition

The MznLnx Exam Prep is your link from the texbook and lecture to your exams.
The MznLnx Exam Preps are unauthorized and comprehensive reviews of your textbooks.

All material provided by MznLnx and Rico Publications (c) 2010
Textbook publishers and textbook authors do not particpate in or contribute to these reviews.

MznLnx

Rico Publications

Exam Prep for Financial Markets & Institutions
3rd Edition
Saunders & Cornett

Publisher: Raymond Houge
Assistant Editor: Michael Rouger
Text and Cover Designer: Lisa Buckner
Marketing Manager: Sara Swagger
Project Manager, Editorial Production: Jerry Emerson
Art Director: Vernon Lowerui

Product Manager: Dave Mason
Editorial Assitant: Rachel Guzmanji
Pedagogy: Debra Long
Cover Image: Jim Reed/Getty Images
Text and Cover Printer: City Printing, Inc.
Compositor: Media Mix, Inc.

(c) 2010 Rico Publications
ALL RIGHTS RESERVED. No part of this work covered by the copyright may be reproduced or used in any form or by an means--graphic, electronic, or mechanical, including photocopying, recording, taping, Web distribution, information storage, and retrieval systems, or in any other manner--without the written permission of the publisher.

Printed in the United States
ISBN:

For more information about our products, contact us at:
Dave.Mason@RicoPublications.com

For permission to use material from this text or product, submit a request online to:
Dave.Mason@RicoPublications.com

Contents

CHAPTER 1
Introduction   1
CHAPTER 2
Determination of Interest Rates   6
CHAPTER 3
Interest Rates and Security Valuation   14
CHAPTER 4
The Federal Reserve System, Monetary Policy, and Interest Rates   18
CHAPTER 5
Money Markets   23
CHAPTER 6
Bond Markets   28
CHAPTER 7
Mortgage Markets   37
CHAPTER 8
Foreign Exchange Markets   45
CHAPTER 9
Stock Markets   51
CHAPTER 10
Derivative Securities Markets   62
CHAPTER 11
Commercial Banks: Industry Overview   72
CHAPTER 12
Commercial Banks`Financial Statements and Analysis   80
CHAPTER 13
Regulation of Commercial Banks   87
CHAPTER 14
Other Lending Institutions: Savings Institutions, Credit Unions   91
CHAPTER 15
Insurance Companies   95
CHAPTER 16
Securities Firms and Investment Banks   98
CHAPTER 17
Mutual Funds   102
CHAPTER 18
Pension Funds   108
CHAPTER 19
Types of Risks Incurred by Financial Institutions   111
CHAPTER 20
Managing Credit Risk on the Balance Sheet   117

Contents (Cont.)

CHAPTER 21
Managing Liquidity Risk on the Balance Sheet — 128

CHAPTER 22
Managing Interest Rate Risk and Insolvency Risk on the Balance Sheet — 132

CHAPTER 23
Managing Risk with Derivative Securities — 135

CHAPTER 24
Managing Risk With Loan Sales and Securitization — 141

ANSWER KEY — 147

TO THE STUDENT

COMPREHENSIVE

The *MznLnx* Exam Prep series is designed to help you pass your exams. Editors at MznLnx review your textbooks and then prepare these practice exams to help you master the textbook material. Unlike study guides, workbooks, and practice tests provided by the texbook publisher and textbook authors, *MznLnx* gives you **all** of the material in each chapter in exam form, not just samples, so you can be sure to nail your exam.

MECHANICAL

The MznLnx Exam Prep series creates exams that will help you learn the subject matter as well as test you on your understanding. Each question is designed to help you master the concept. Just working through the exams, you gain an understanding of the subject--its a simple mechanical process that produces success.

INTEGRATED STUDY GUIDE AND REVIEW

MznLnx is not just a set of exams designed to test you, its also a comprehensive review of the subject content. Each exam question is also a review of the concept, making sure that you will get the answer correct without having to go to other sources of material. You learn as you go! Its the easiest way to pass an exam.

HUMOR

Studying can be tedious and dry. MznLnx's instructional design includes moderate humor within the exam questions on occassion, to break the tedium and revitalize the brain

Chapter 1. Introduction

1. _____ is the provision of resources (such as granting a loan) by one party to another party where that second party does not reimburse the first party immediately, thereby generating a debt, and instead arranges either to repay or return those resources (or material(s) of equal value) at a later date. The first party is called a creditor, also known as a lender, while the second party is called a debtor, also known as a borrower.

Movements of financial capital are normally dependent on either _____ or equity transfers.

- a. Clearing house
- b. Comparable
- c. Warrant
- d. Credit

2. _____, is when a company issues common stock or shares to the public for the first time. They are often issued by smaller, younger companies seeking capital to expand, but can also be done by large privately-owned companies looking to become publicly traded.

In an _____ the issuer may obtain the assistance of an underwriting firm, which helps it determine what type of security to issue (common or preferred), best offering price and time to bring it to market.

- a. Initial public offering
- b. Insolvency
- c. Asian Financial Crisis
- d. Interest

3. The _____ is that part of the capital markets that deals with the issuance of new securities. Companies, governments or public sector institutions can obtain funding through the sale of a new stock or bond issue. This is typically done through a syndicate of securities dealers.

- a. Peer group analysis
- b. Sector rotation
- c. Volatility clustering
- d. Primary market

4. In financial accounting, the term _____ is most commonly used to describe any part of shareholders' equity, except for basic share capital. Sometimes, the term is used instead of the term provision; such a use, however, is inconsistent with the terminology suggested by International Accounting Standards Board. For more information about provisions, see provision (accounting.)

- a. Treasury stock
- b. Reserve
- c. FIFO and LIFO accounting
- d. Closing entries

5. The _____ is the financial market where previously issued securities and financial instruments such as stock, bonds, options, and futures are bought and sold. The term '_____' is also used refer to the market for any used goods or assets, or an alternative use for an existing product or asset where the customer base is the second market

With primary issuances of securities or financial instruments, or the primary market, investors purchase these securities directly from issuers such as corporations issuing shares in an IPO or private placement, or directly from the federal government in the case of treasuries.

- a. Financial market
- b. Performance attribution
- c. Delta neutral
- d. Secondary market

6. The _____ is the market for securities, where companies and governments can raise longterm funds. The _____ includes the stock market and the bond market. Financial regulators, such as the U.S. Securities and Exchange Commission, oversee the _____s in their designated countries to ensure that investors are protected against fraud.

a. Delta neutral
c. Capital market
b. Forward market
d. Spot rate

7. In finance, a _____ is a debt security, in which the authorized issuer owes the holders a debt and, depending on the terms of the _____, is obliged to pay interest (the coupon) and/or to repay the principal at a later date, termed maturity.

Thus a _____ is a loan: the issuer is the borrower, the _____ holder is the lender, and the coupon is the interest. _____s provide the borrower with external funds to finance long-term investments, or, in the case of government _____s, to finance current expenditure.

a. Bond
c. Puttable bond
b. Catastrophe bonds
d. Convertible bond

8. A _____ is a bond issued by a corporation. The term is usually applied to longer-term debt instruments, generally with a maturity date falling at least a year after their issue date. (The term 'commercial paper' is sometimes used for instruments with a shorter maturity.)

a. Corporate bond
c. Serial bond
b. Brady bonds
d. Government bond

9. A _____ is a fungible, negotiable instrument representing financial value. They are broadly categorized into debt securities (such as banknotes, bonds and debentures), and equity securities; e.g., common stocks. The company or other entity issuing the _____ is called the issuer.

a. Security
c. Securities lending
b. Tracking stock
d. Book entry

10. The U.S. _____ is an independent agency of the United States government which holds primary responsibility for enforcing the federal securities laws and regulating the securities industry, the nation's stock and options exchanges, and other electronic securities markets. The SEC was created by section 4 of the SEC of 1934 (now codified as 15 U.S.C. Â§ 78d and commonly referred to as the 1934 Act.)

a. 7-Eleven
c. 4-4-5 Calendar
b. 529 plan
d. Securities and Exchange Commission

11. A _____ is a financial contract whose value is derived from the value of something else (known as the underlying.) The underlying on which a _____ is based can be an asset, weather conditions bonds or other forms of credit.

a. 4-4-5 Calendar
c. Derivative
b. 7-Eleven
d. 529 plan

12. _____ is the discipline of identifying, monitoring and limiting risks. In some cases the acceptable risk may be near zero. Risks can come from accidents, natural causes and disasters as well as deliberate attacks from an adversary.

a. Risk management
c. 4-4-5 Calendar
b. Penny stock
d. FIFO

13. _____ is a measure of the ability of a debtor to pay their debts as and when they fall due. It is usually expressed as a ratio or a percentage of current liabilities.

For a corporation with a published balance sheet there are various ratios used to calculate a measure of liquidity.

   a. Operating profit margin
   b. Accounting liquidity
   c. Invested capital
   d. Operating leverage

14. In economics, business, and accounting, a _____ is the value of money that has been used up to produce something, and hence is not available for use anymore. In business, the _____ may be one of acquisition, in which case the amount of money expended to acquire it is counted as _____. In this case, money is the input that is gone in order to acquire the thing.
   a. Marginal cost
   b. Sliding scale fees
   c. Cost
   d. Fixed costs

15. In business and accounting, _____s are everything of value that is owned by a person or company. The balance sheet of a firm records the monetary value of the _____s owned by the firm. The two major _____ classes are tangible _____s and intangible _____s.
   a. Income
   b. EBITDA
   c. Accounts payable
   d. Asset

16. _____ in finance is a risk management technique, related to hedging, that mixes a wide variety of investments within a portfolio. Because the fluctuations of a single security have less impact on a diverse portfolio, _____ minimizes the risk from any one investment.

A simple example of _____ is the following: On a particular island the entire economy consists of two companies: one that sells umbrellas and another that sells sunscreen.

   a. 4-4-5 Calendar
   b. Diversification
   c. 7-Eleven
   d. 529 plan

17. _____, in microeconomics, are the cost advantages that a business obtains due to expansion. _____ may be utilized by any size firm expanding its scale of operation.
   a. Uniform Commercial Code
   b. Employee Retirement Income Security Act
   c. Economies of scale
   d. Articles of incorporation

18. In the United States, a _____ is an offering of securities that are not registered with the Securities and Exchange Commission (SEC.) Such offerings exploit an exemption offered by the Securities Act of 1933 that comes with several restrictions, including a prohibition against general solicitation. This exemption allows companies to avoid quarterly reporting requirements and many of the legal liabilities associated with the Sarbanes-Oxley Act.
   a. Private placement
   b. 529 plan
   c. 4-4-5 Calendar
   d. 7-Eleven

19. _____ is the process by which the government, or monetary authority of a country controls (i) the supply of money central bank (ii) availability of money, and (iii) cost of money or rate of interest, in order to attain a set of objectives oriented towards the growth and stability of the economy. Monetary theory provides insight into how to craft optimal _____.

_____ is referred to as either being an expansionary policy where an expansionary policy increases the total supply of money in the economy, and a contractionary policy decreases the total money supply.

   a. Federal Open Market Committee   b. Natural resources consumption tax
   c. Tax exemption   d. Monetary policy

20. _____s are deposits denominated in United States dollars at banks outside the United States, and thus are not under the jurisdiction of the Federal Reserve. Consequently, such deposits are subject to much less regulation than similar deposits within the United States, allowing for higher margins. There is nothing 'European' about _____ deposits; a US dollar-denominated deposit in Tokyo or Caracas would likewise be deemed _____ deposits.

   a. ABN Amro   b. A Random Walk Down Wall Street
   c. AAB   d. Eurodollar

21. A _____ is an exchange of promises between two or more parties to do an act which is enforceable in a court of law. It is where an unqualified offer meets a qualified acceptance and the parties reach Consensus ad Idem. The parties must have the necessary capacity to _____ and the _____ must not be either trifling, indeterminate, impossible or illegal.

   a. 4-4-5 Calendar   b. 529 plan
   c. 7-Eleven   d. Contract

22. In finance, a _____ is a standardized contract, to buy or sell a specified commodity of standardized quality at a certain date in the future, at a market determined price (the futures price.)

The price is determined by the instantaneous equilibrium between the forces of supply and demand among competing buy and sell orders on the exchange at the time of the purchase or sale of the contract.

In many cases, the items may be such non-traditional 'commodities' as foreign currencies, commercial or government paper [e.g., bonds], or 'baskets' of corporate equity ['stock indices'] or other financial instruments.

   a. Heston model   b. Financial future
   c. Futures contract   d. Repurchase agreement

23. An _____ is a contract written by a seller that conveys to the buyer the right -- but not the obligation -- to buy (in the case of a call _____) or to sell (in the case of a put _____) a particular asset, such as a piece of property such as, among others, a futures contract. In return for granting the _____, the seller collects a payment (the premium) from the buyer.

For example, buying a call _____ provides the right to buy a specified quantity of a security at a set strike price at some time on or before expiration, while buying a put _____ provides the right to sell.

   a. Amortization   b. AT'T Mobility LLC
   c. Option   d. Annuity

Chapter 1. Introduction

24. The institution most often referenced by the word '_____' is a public or publicly traded _____, the shares of which are traded on a public stock exchange (e.g., the New York Stock Exchange or Nasdaq in the United States) where shares of stock of _____s are bought and sold by and to the general public. Most of the largest businesses in the world are publicly traded _____s. However, the majority of _____s are said to be closely held, privately held or close _____s, meaning that no ready market exists for the trading of shares.
   a. Corporation
   b. Federal Home Loan Mortgage Corporation
   c. Depository Trust Company
   d. Protect

25. _____ is a stock market index for the Tokyo Stock Exchange (TSE.) It has been calculated daily by the Nihon Keizai Shimbun (Nikkei) newspaper since 1950. It is a price-weighted average (the unit is Yen), and the components are reviewed once a year.
   a. 529 plan
   b. 4-4-5 Calendar
   c. Nikkei 225
   d. 7-Eleven

26. A _____, securities exchange or (in Europe) bourse is a corporation or mutual organization which provides 'trading' facilities for stock brokers and traders, to trade stocks and other securities. _____s also provide facilities for the issue and redemption of securities as well as other financial instruments and capital events including the payment of income and dividends. The securities traded on a _____ include: shares issued by companies, unit trusts and other pooled investment products and bonds.
   a. 529 plan
   b. 7-Eleven
   c. Stock Exchange
   d. 4-4-5 Calendar

Chapter 2. Determination of Interest Rates

1. In economics, the _____ is the proposition by Irving Fisher that the real interest rate is independent of monetary measures, especially the nominal interest rate. The Fisher equation is

$$r_r = r_n >- >\pi^e.$$

This means, the real interest rate (r_r) equals the nominal interest rate (r_n) minus expected rate of inflation ($>\pi^e$.) Here all the rates are continuously compounded.

   a. 529 plan
   b. 4-4-5 Calendar
   c. Fisher hypothesis
   d. 7-Eleven

2. In finance and economics _____ refers to the rate of interest before adjustment for inflation (in contrast with the real interest rate); or, for interest balls stated' without adjustment for the full effect of compounding (also referred to as the nominal annual rate.) An interest rate is called nominal if the frequency of compounding (e.g. a month) is not identical to the basic time unit (normally a year.)

The real interest rate includes compensation for the lender's lost value due to inflation, whereas the _____ excludes inflation.

   a. SIBOR
   b. Cash accumulation equation
   c. Shanghai Interbank Offered Rate
   d. Nominal interest rate

3. _____ is a fee paid on borrowed assets. It is the price paid for the use of borrowed money, or, money earned by deposited funds. Assets that are sometimes lent with _____ include money, shares, consumer goods through hire purchase, major assets such as aircraft, and even entire factories in finance lease arrangements.
   a. Insolvency
   b. Interest
   c. AAB
   d. A Random Walk Down Wall Street

4. An _____ is the price a borrower pays for the use of money they do not own, and the return a lender receives for deferring the use of funds, by lending it to the borrower. _____s are normally expressed as a percentage rate over the period of one year.

_____s targets are also a vital tool of monetary policy and are used to control variables like investment, inflation, and unemployment.

   a. ABN Amro
   b. AAB
   c. A Random Walk Down Wall Street
   d. Interest rate

5. In finance, the value of an option consists of two components, its intrinsic value and its _____. Time value is simply the difference between option value and intrinsic value. _____ is also known as theta, extrinsic value, or instrumental value.
   a. Debt buyer
   b. Time value
   c. Conservatism
   d. Global Squeeze

Chapter 2. Determination of Interest Rates 7

6. Simply put, _____ is the value of money figuring in a given amount of interest for a given amount of time. For example 100 dollars of todays money held for a year at 5 percent interest is worth 105 dollars, therefore 100 dollars paid now or 105 dollars paid exactly one year from now is the same amount of payment of money with that given intersest at that given amount of time. This notion dates at least to Martín de Azpilcueta of the School of Salamanca.

All of the standard calculations for _____ derive from the most basic algebraic expression for the present value of a future sum, 'discounted' to the present by an amount equal to the _____. For example, a sum of FV to be received in one year is discounted (at the rate of interest r) to give a sum of PV at present: PV = FV -- rÂ·PV = FV/(1+r).

   a. Time value of money   b. Current account
   c. Zero-coupon bond   d. Coefficient of variation

7. _____ is the concept of adding accumulated interest back to the principal, so that interest is earned on interest from that moment on. The act of declaring interest to be principal is called compounding (i.e., interest is compounded.) A loan, for example, may have its interest compounded every month: in this case, a loan with $100 principal and 1% interest per month would have a balance of $101 at the end of the first month.

   a. Risk management   b. Penny stock
   c. 4-4-5 Calendar   d. Compound interest

8. _____ measures the nominal future sum of money that a given sum of money is 'worth' at a specified time in the future assuming a certain interest rate rate of return; it is the present value multiplied by the accumulation function.

The value does not include corrections for inflation or other factors that affect the true value of money in the future. This is used in time value of money calculations.

   a. Present value of costs   b. Future-oriented
   c. Discounted cash flow   d. Future value

9. _____ is the value on a given date of a future payment or series of future payments, discounted to reflect the time value of money and other factors such as investment risk. _____ calculations are widely used in business and economics to provide a means to compare cash flows at different times on a meaningful 'like to like' basis.

The most commonly applied model of the time value of money is compound interest.

   a. Present value   b. Present value of benefits
   c. Negative gearing   d. Net present value

10. In finance, _____ is the process of estimating the potential market value of a financial asset or liability. they can be done on assets (for example, investments in marketable securities such as stocks, options, business enterprises, or intangible assets such as patents and trademarks) or on liabilities (e.g., Bonds issued by a company.) _____s are required in many contexts including investment analysis, capital budgeting, merger and acquisition transactions, financial reporting, taxable events to determine the proper tax liability, and in litigation.

   a. Procter ' Gamble   b. Share
   c. Margin   d. Valuation

Chapter 2. Determination of Interest Rates

11. An _____ can be defined as a contract which provides an income stream in return for an initial payment.

An immediate _____ is an _____ for which the time between the contract date and the date of the first payment is not longer than the time interval between payments. A common use for an immediate _____ is to provide a pension to a retired person or persons.

    a. Annuity   b. Intrinsic value
    c. AT'T Inc.   d. Amortization

12. _____ is that which is owed; usually referencing assets owed, but the term can cover other obligations. In the case of assets, _____ is a means of using future purchasing power in the present before a summation has been earned. Some companies and corporations use _____ as a part of their overall corporate finance strategy.
    a. Credit cycle   b. Partial Payment
    c. Cross-collateralization   d. Debt

13. _____ is the discipline of identifying, monitoring and limiting risks. In some cases the acceptable risk may be near zero. Risks can come from accidents, natural causes and disasters as well as deliberate attacks from an adversary.
    a. Penny stock   b. 4-4-5 Calendar
    c. Risk management   d. FIFO

14. In business and accounting, _____s are everything of value that is owned by a person or company. The balance sheet of a firm records the monetary value of the _____s owned by the firm. The two major _____ classes are tangible _____s and intangible _____s.
    a. Asset   b. EBITDA
    c. Accounts payable   d. Income

15. In economics, _____ is a measure of the relative satisfaction from or desirability of consumption of various goods and services. Given this measure, one may speak meaningfully of increasing or decreasing _____, and thereby explain economic behavior in terms of attempts to increase one's _____. For illustrative purposes, changes in _____ are sometimes expressed in units called utils.
    a. A Random Walk Down Wall Street   b. Utility function
    c. Utility   d. AAB

16. A _____ is a measure of the average price of consumer goods and services purchased by households. The _____ can be used to index (i.e., adjust for the effects of inflation) wages, salaries, pensions, or regulated or contracted prices. The _____ is, along with the population census and the National Income and Product Accounts, one of the most closely watched national economic statistics.
    a. 4-4-5 Calendar   b. 529 plan
    c. Divisia index   d. Consumer price index

17. In economics, _____ is a rise in the general level of prices of goods and services in an economy over a period of time. The term '_____' once referred to increases in the money supply (monetary _____); however, economic debates about the relationship between money supply and price levels have led to its primary use today in describing price _____. _____ can also be described as a decline in the real value of money--a loss of purchasing power in the medium of exchange which is also the monetary unit of account.

a. ABN Amro
b. AAB
c. A Random Walk Down Wall Street
d. Inflation

18. The '_____' is approximately the nominal interest rate minus the inflation rate Since the inflation rate over the course of a loan is not known initially, volatility in inflation represents a risk to both the lender and the borrower.

In economics and finance, an individual who lends money for repayment at a later point in time expects to be compensated for the time value of money, or not having the use of that money while it is lent.

a. 4-4-5 Calendar
b. 7-Eleven
c. 529 plan
d. Real interest rate

19. A _____ is a normalized average (typically a weighted average) of prices for a given class of goods or services in a given region, during a given interval of time. It is a statistic designed to help to compare how these prices, taken as a whole, differ between time periods or geographical locations.

a. Transfer pricing
b. Discounts and allowances
c. Price discrimination
d. Price index

20. _____ is the provision of resources (such as granting a loan) by one party to another party where that second party does not reimburse the first party immediately, thereby generating a debt, and instead arranges either to repay or return those resources (or material(s) of equal value) at a later date. The first party is called a creditor, also known as a lender, while the second party is called a debtor, also known as a borrower.

Movements of financial capital are normally dependent on either _____ or equity transfers.

a. Clearing house
b. Warrant
c. Comparable
d. Credit

21. _____ is the risk of loss due to a debtor's non-payment of a loan or other line of credit (either the principal or interest (coupon) or both)

Most lenders employ their own models (credit scorecards) to rank potential and existing customers according to risk, and then apply appropriate strategies. With products such as unsecured personal loans or mortgages, lenders charge a higher price for higher risk customers and vice versa. With revolving products such as credit cards and overdrafts, risk is controlled through careful setting of credit limits.

a. Credit risk
b. Transaction risk
c. Market risk
d. Liquidity risk

22. In finance, _____ occurs when a debtor has not met its legal obligations according to the debt contract, e.g. it has not made a scheduled payment, or has violated a loan covenant (condition) of the debt contract. _____ may occur if the debtor is either unwilling or unable to pay their debt. This can occur with all debt obligations including bonds, mortgages, loans, and promissory notes.

a. Credit crunch
b. Debt validation
c. Vendor finance
d. Default

Chapter 2. Determination of Interest Rates

23. _____ is a measure of the ability of a debtor to pay their debts as and when they fall due. It is usually expressed as a ratio or a percentage of current liabilities.

For a corporation with a published balance sheet there are various ratios used to calculate a measure of liquidity.

a. Operating profit margin
b. Invested capital
c. Operating leverage
d. Accounting liquidity

24. _____ arises from situations in which a party interested in trading an asset cannot do it because nobody in the market wants to trade that asset. _____ becomes particularly important to parties who are about to hold or currently hold an asset, since it affects their ability to trade.

Manifestation of _____ is very different from a drop of price to zero.

a. Credit risk
b. Liquidity risk
c. Tracking error
d. Currency risk

25. In financial accounting, a _____ or statement of financial position is a summary of a person's or organization's balances. Assets, liabilities and ownership equity are listed as of a specific date, such as the end of its financial year. A _____ is often described as a snapshot of a company's financial condition.

a. Statement of retained earnings
b. Statement on Auditing Standards No. 70: Service Organizations
c. Financial statements
d. Balance sheet

26.

In finance, the _____ can be the expected rate of return above the risk-free interest rate. When measuring risk, a common sense approach is to compare the risk-free return on T-bills and the very risky return on other investments. The difference between these two returns can be interpreted as a measure of the excess return on the average risky asset. This excess return is known as the _____.

a. Risk premium
b. Risk adjusted return on capital
c. Risk aversion
d. Risk modeling

27. In finance, a _____ is a type of bond that can be converted into shares of stock in the issuing company, usually at some pre-announced ratio. It is a hybrid security with debt- and equity-like features. Although it typically has a low coupon rate, the holder is compensated with the ability to convert the bond to common stock, usually at a substantial discount to the stock's market value.

a. Bond fund
b. Corporate bond
c. Convertible bond
d. Gilts

28. A _____, in its most general sense, is a solemn promise to engage in or refrain from a specified action.

Chapter 2. Determination of Interest Rates 11

More specifically, a _____, in contrast to a contract, is a one-way agreement whereby the _____er is the only party bound by the promise. A _____ may have conditions and prerequisites that qualify the undertaking, including the actions of second or third parties, but there is no inherent agreement by such other parties to fulfill those requirements.

- a. Covenant
- b. Federal Trade Commission Act
- c. Clayton Antitrust Act
- d. Partnership

29. In financial accounting, _____s are precautions for which the amount or probability of occurrence are not known. Typical examples are _____s for warranty costs and _____ for taxes the term reserve is used instead of term _____; such a use, however, is inconsistent with the terminology suggested by International Accounting Standards Board.
- a. Petty cash
- b. Momentum Accounting and Triple-Entry Bookkeeping
- c. Provision
- d. Money measurement concept

30. A _____ is a fungible, negotiable instrument representing financial value. They are broadly categorized into debt securities (such as banknotes, bonds and debentures), and equity securities; e.g., common stocks. The company or other entity issuing the _____ is called the issuer.
- a. Security
- b. Securities lending
- c. Book entry
- d. Tracking stock

31. _____ is a life of security. It may also refer to the final payment date of a loan or other financial instrument, at which point all remaining interest and principal is due to be paid.

1, 3, 6 months _____ band can be calculated by using 30-day per month periods.

- a. Primary market
- b. Replacement cost
- c. False billing
- d. Maturity

32. In finance, the term _____ describes the amount in cash that returns to the owners of a security. Normally it does not include the price variations, at the difference of the total return. _____ applies to various stated rates of return on stocks (common and preferred, and convertible), fixed income instruments (bonds, notes, bills, strips, zero coupon), and some other investment type insurance products (e.g. annuities.)
- a. Yield to maturity
- b. 4-4-5 Calendar
- c. Yield
- d. Macaulay duration

33. In finance, the _____ is the relation between the interest rate (or cost of borrowing) and the time to maturity of the debt for a given borrower in a given currency. For example, the current U.S. dollar interest rates paid on U.S. Treasury securities for various maturities are closely watched by many traders, and are commonly plotted on a graph such as the one on the right which is informally called 'the _____.' More formal mathematical descriptions of this relation are often called the term structure of interest rates.

The yield of a debt instrument is the annualized percentage increase in the value of the investment.

Chapter 2. Determination of Interest Rates

a. Yield curve
b. 4-4-5 Calendar
c. 529 plan
d. 7-Eleven

34. In finance, the yield curve is the relation between the interest rate (or cost of borrowing) and the time to maturity of the debt for a given borrower in a given currency. For example, the current U.S. dollar interest rates paid on U.S. Treasury securities for various maturities are closely watched by many traders, and are commonly plotted on a graph such as the one on the right which is informally called 'the yield curve.' More formal mathematical descriptions of this relation are often called the _____.

The yield of a debt instrument is the annualized percentage increase in the value of the investment.

a. 529 plan
b. 7-Eleven
c. 4-4-5 Calendar
d. Term structure of interest rates

35. _____ is a term used to explain a difference between two types of financial securities (e.g. stocks), that have all the same qualities except liquidity. For example:

_____ is a segment of a three-part theory that works to explain the behavior of yield curves for interest rates. The upwards-curving component of the interest yield can be explained by the _____.

a. 4-4-5 Calendar
b. 529 plan
c. 7-Eleven
d. Liquidity premium

36. The _____ or forward rate is the agreed upon price of an asset in a forward contract. Using the rational pricing assumption, we can express the _____ in terms of the spot price and any dividends etc., so that there is no possibility for arbitrage.

The _____ is given by:

$$\boxed{}_>$$

where

F is the _____ to be paid at time T
e^x is the exponential function
r is the risk-free interest rate
q is the cost-of-carry
S_0 is the spot price of the asset (i.e. what it would sell for at time 0)
D_i is a dividend which is guaranteed to be paid at time t_i where $0 < t_i < T$.

The two questions here are what price the short position (the seller of the asset) should offer to maximize his gain, and what price the long position (the buyer of the asset) should accept to maximize his gain?

At the very least we know that both do not want to lose any money in the deal.

a. Financial Gerontology
c. Security interest

b. Biweekly Mortgage
d. Forward price

Chapter 3. Interest Rates and Security Valuation

1. The coupon or _____ of a bond is the amount of interest paid per year expressed as a percentage of the face value of the bond.

For example if you hold $10,000 nominal of a bond described as a 4.5% loan stock, you will receive $450 in interest each year (probably in two installments of $225 each.)

Not all bonds have coupons.

   a. Zero-coupon bond
   c. Coupon rate
   b. Revenue bonds
   d. Puttable bond

2. _____ is a fee paid on borrowed assets. It is the price paid for the use of borrowed money, or, money earned by deposited funds. Assets that are sometimes lent with _____ include money, shares, consumer goods through hire purchase, major assets such as aircraft, and even entire factories in finance lease arrangements.
   a. AAB
   c. A Random Walk Down Wall Street
   b. Insolvency
   d. Interest

3. An _____ is the price a borrower pays for the use of money they do not own, and the return a lender receives for deferring the use of funds, by lending it to the borrower. _____s are normally expressed as a percentage rate over the period of one year.

_____s targets are also a vital tool of monetary policy and are used to control variables like investment, inflation, and unemployment.

   a. ABN Amro
   c. A Random Walk Down Wall Street
   b. AAB
   d. Interest rate

4. In finance, _____, also known as return on investment is the ratio of money gained or lost on an investment relative to the amount of money invested. The amount of money gained or lost may be referred to as interest, profit/loss, gain/loss, or net income/loss. The money invested may be referred to as the asset, capital, principal, or the cost basis of the investment.
   a. Composiition of Creditors
   c. Stock or scrip dividends
   b. Doctrine of the Proper Law
   d. Rate of return

5. _____ is the value on a given date of a future payment or series of future payments, discounted to reflect the time value of money and other factors such as investment risk. _____ calculations are widely used in business and economics to provide a means to compare cash flows at different times on a meaningful 'like to like' basis.

The most commonly applied model of the time value of money is compound interest.

   a. Present value
   c. Negative gearing
   b. Present value of benefits
   d. Net present value

6. In finance, a _____ is a debt security, in which the authorized issuer owes the holders a debt and, depending on the terms of the _____, is obliged to pay interest (the coupon) and/or to repay the principal at a later date, termed maturity.

Chapter 3. Interest Rates and Security Valuation

Thus a _____ is a loan: the issuer is the borrower, the _____ holder is the lender, and the coupon is the interest. _____s provide the borrower with external funds to finance long-term investments, or, in the case of government _____s, to finance current expenditure.

- a. Convertible bond
- b. Puttable bond
- c. Catastrophe bonds
- d. Bond

7. _____ is the process of determining the fair price of a bond. As with any security or capital investment, the fair value of a bond is the present value of the stream of cash flows it is expected to generate. Hence, the price or value of a bond is determined by discounting the bond's expected cash flows to the present using the appropriate discount rate.
- a. Bond fund
- b. Catastrophe bonds
- c. Collateralized debt obligations
- d. Bond valuation

8. In finance, the _____ of a financial asset measures the sensitivity of the asset's price to interest rate movements, expressed as a number of years. The reason for expressing this sensitivity in years is that the time that will elapse until a cash flow is received allows more interest to accumulate. Therefore the price of an asset with long term cashflows has more interest rate sensitivity than an asset with cashflows in the near future.
- a. Yield to maturity
- b. Macaulay duration
- c. 4-4-5 Calendar
- d. Duration

9. A _____ is a bond bought at a price lower than its face value, with the face value repaid at the time of maturity. It does not make periodic interest payments, or have so-called 'coupons,' hence the term _____. Investors earn return from the compounded interest all paid at maturity plus the difference between the discounted price of the bond and its par value.
- a. Clean price
- b. Bond fund
- c. Corporate bond
- d. Zero-coupon bond

10. _____ is the balance of the amounts of cash being received and paid by a business during a defined period of time, sometimes tied to a specific project. Measurement of _____ can be used

- to evaluate the state or performance of a business or project.
- to determine problems with liquidity. Being profitable does not necessarily mean being liquid. A company can fail because of a shortage of cash, even while profitable.
- to generate project rate of returns. The time of _____s into and out of projects are used as inputs to financial models such as internal rate of return, and net present value.
- to examine income or growth of a business when it is believed that accrual accounting concepts do not represent economic realities. Alternately, _____ can be used to 'validate' the net income generated by accrual accounting.

_____ as a generic term may be used differently depending on context, and certain _____ definitions may be adapted by analysts and users for their own uses. Common terms include operating _____ and free _____.

_____s can be classified into:

1. Operational _____s: Cash received or expended as a result of the company's core business activities.
2. Investment _____s: Cash received or expended through capital expenditure, investments or acquisitions.
3. Financing _____s: Cash received or expended as a result of financial activities, such as interests and dividends.

All three together - the net _____ - are necessary to reconcile the beginning cash balance to the ending cash balance. Loan draw downs or equity injections, that is just shifting of capital but no expenditure as such, are not considered in the net _____.

a. Corporate finance
b. Shareholder value
c. Real option
d. Cash flow

11. In finance, _____ is the process of estimating the potential market value of a financial asset or liability. they can be done on assets (for example, investments in marketable securities such as stocks, options, business enterprises, or intangible assets such as patents and trademarks) or on liabilities (e.g., Bonds issued by a company.) _____s are required in many contexts including investment analysis, capital budgeting, merger and acquisition transactions, financial reporting, taxable events to determine the proper tax liability, and in litigation.

a. Share
b. Procter ' Gamble
c. Margin
d. Valuation

12. A '_____' is a 'Charge' that is paid to obtain the right to delay a payment. Essentially, the payer purchases the right to make a given payment in the future instead of in the Present. The '_____', or 'Charge' that must be paid to delay the payment, is simply the difference between what the payment amount would be if it were paid in the present and what the payment amount would be paid if it were paid in the future.

a. Discount
b. Value at risk
c. Risk modeling
d. Risk aversion

13. A _____ is a bond bought at a price lower than its face value, with the face value repaid at the time of maturity. It does not make periodic interest payments, or so-called 'coupons,' hence the term zero-coupon bond. Investors earn return from the compounded interest all paid at maturity plus the difference between the discounted price of the bond and its par value.

a. Zero coupon bond
b. Bowie bonds
c. Municipal bond
d. Callable bond

14. A _____ is a generic term for any bond selling for more than 100% of par value, i.e., at a price greater than 100.00, which typically occurs for high coupon bonds in a falling interest rate climate.

a. Municipal bond
b. Premium bond
c. Revenue bonds
d. Nominal yield

15. _____, in finance and accounting, means stated value or face value. From this comes the expressions at par (at the _____), over par (over _____) and under par (under _____.)

The term '_____' has several meanings depending on context and geography.

a. Par value
b. FIDC
c. Sinking fund
d. Global Squeeze

16. In finance, the term _____ describes the amount in cash that returns to the owners of a security. Normally it does not include the price variations, at the difference of the total return. _____ applies to various stated rates of return on stocks (common and preferred, and convertible), fixed income instruments (bonds, notes, bills, strips, zero coupon), and some other investment type insurance products (e.g. annuities.)

a. Yield to maturity
b. Macaulay duration
c. 4-4-5 Calendar
d. Yield

17. The _____ or redemption yield is the yield promised to the bondholder on the assumption that the bond or other fixed-interest security such as gilts will be held to maturity, that all coupon and principal payments will be made and coupon payments are reinvested at the bond's promised yield at the same rate as invested. It is a measure of the return of the bond. This technique in theory allows investors to calculate the fair value of different financial instruments.

a. Macaulay duration
b. Yield
c. 4-4-5 Calendar
d. Yield to maturity

18. _____ is a life of security. It may also refer to the final payment date of a loan or other financial instrument, at which point all remaining interest and principal is due to be paid.

1, 3, 6 months _____ band can be calculated by using 30-day per month periods.

a. False billing
b. Replacement cost
c. Primary market
d. Maturity

19. In economics, the _____ is the proposition by Irving Fisher that the real interest rate is independent of monetary measures, especially the nominal interest rate. The Fisher equation is

$r_r = r_n >- >\pi^e$.

This means, the real interest rate (r_r) equals the nominal interest rate (r_n) minus expected rate of inflation ($>\pi^e$.) Here all the rates are continuously compounded.

a. 7-Eleven
b. 4-4-5 Calendar
c. Fisher hypothesis
d. 529 plan

20. A _____ is a fungible, negotiable instrument representing financial value. They are broadly categorized into debt securities (such as banknotes, bonds and debentures), and equity securities; e.g., common stocks. The company or other entity issuing the _____ is called the issuer.

a. Tracking stock
b. Book entry
c. Securities lending
d. Security

Chapter 4. The Federal Reserve System, Monetary Policy, and Interest Rates

1. The _____ , a component of the Federal Reserve System, is charged under United States law with overseeing the nation's open market operations. It is the Federal Reserve Committee that makes key decisions about interest rates and the growth jam of the United States money supply. It is the principal organ of United States national monetary policy.
    a. Fiscal policy
    b. Tax incidence
    c. Tax exemption
    d. Federal Open Market Committee

2. In financial accounting, the term _____ is most commonly used to describe any part of shareholders' equity, except for basic share capital. Sometimes, the term is used instead of the term provision; such a use, however, is inconsistent with the terminology suggested by International Accounting Standards Board. For more information about provisions, see provision (accounting.)
    a. Closing entries
    b. Treasury stock
    c. FIFO and LIFO accounting
    d. Reserve

3. A _____ or bank is a financial institution whose primary activity is to act as a payment agent for customers and to borrow and lend money.

The first modern bank was founded in Italy in Genoa in 1406, its name was Banco di San Giorgio (Bank of St. George.)

Many other financial activities were added over time.

    a. 4-4-5 Calendar
    b. Black Sea Trade and Development Bank
    c. Bought deal
    d. Banker

4. A _____, reserve bank, or monetary authority is the entity responsible for the monetary policy of a country or of a group of member states. It is a bank that can lend money to other banks in times of need. Its primary responsibility is to maintain the stability of the national currency and money supply, but more active duties include controlling subsidized-loan interest rates, and acting as a lender of last resort to the banking sector during times of financial crisis (private banks often being integral to the national financial system.)
    a. 529 plan
    b. 7-Eleven
    c. 4-4-5 Calendar
    d. Central bank

5. A '_____' is a 'Charge' that is paid to obtain the right to delay a payment. Essentially, the payer purchases the right to make a given payment in the future instead of in the Present. The '_____', or 'Charge' that must be paid to delay the payment, is simply the difference between what the payment amount would be if it were paid in the present and what the payment amount would be paid if it were paid in the future.
    a. Discount
    b. Risk aversion
    c. Value at risk
    d. Risk modeling

6. The _____ is an interest rate a central bank charges depository institutions that borrow reserves from it.

Chapter 4. The Federal Reserve System, Monetary Policy, and Interest Rates   19

The term _____ has two meanings:

- the same as interest rate; the term 'discount' does not refer to the meaning of the word, but to the purpose of using the quantity, such as computations of present value, e.g. net present value / discounted cash flow

- the annual effective _____, which is the annual interest divided by the capital including that interest; this rate is lower than the interest rate; it corresponds to using the value after a year as the nominal value, and seeing the initial value as the nominal value minus a discount; it is used for Treasury Bills and similar financial instruments

The annual effective _____ is the annual interest divided by the capital including that interest, which is the interest rate divided by 100% plus the interest rate. It is the annual discount factor to be applied to the future cash flow, to find the discount, subtracted from a future value to find the value one year earlier.

For example, suppose there is a government bond that sells for $95 and pays $100 in a year's time.

a. Stochastic volatility
c. Fisher equation
b. Black-Scholes
d. Discount rate

7. _____ is the process by which the government, or monetary authority of a country controls (i) the supply of money central bank (ii) availability of money, and (iii) cost of money or rate of interest, in order to attain a set of objectives oriented towards the growth and stability of the economy. Monetary theory provides insight into how to craft optimal _____.

_____ is referred to as either being an expansionary policy where an expansionary policy increases the total supply of money in the economy, and a contractionary policy decreases the total money supply.

a. Natural resources consumption tax
c. Federal Open Market Committee
b. Tax exemption
d. Monetary policy

8. _____ is a stock market index for the Tokyo Stock Exchange (TSE.) It has been calculated daily by the Nihon Keizai Shimbun (Nikkei) newspaper since 1950. It is a price-weighted average (the unit is Yen), and the components are reviewed once a year.
a. 4-4-5 Calendar
c. 7-Eleven
b. 529 plan
d. Nikkei 225

9. In banking and finance, _____ denotes all activities from the time a commitment is made for a transaction until it is settled. _____ is necessary because the speed of trades is much faster than the cycle time for completing the underlying transaction.

In its widest sense _____ involves the management of post-trading, pre-settlement credit exposures, to ensure that trades are settled in accordance with market rules, even if a buyer or seller should become insolvent prior to settlement.

Chapter 4. The Federal Reserve System, Monetary Policy, and Interest Rates

    a. Clearing
    c. Clearing house
    b. Procter ' Gamble
    d. Share

10. A _____ is a financial services company that provides clearing and settlement services for financial transactions, usually on a futures exchange, and often acts as central counterparty (the payor actually pays the _____, which then pays the payee). A _____ may also offer novation, the substitution of a new contract or debt for an old, or other credit enhancement services to its members.

The term is also used for banks like Suffolk Bank that acted as a restraint on the over-issuance of private bank notes.

    a. Bucket shop
    c. Valuation
    b. Warrant
    d. Clearing house

11. In financial accounting, a _____ or statement of financial position is a summary of a person's or organization's balances. Assets, liabilities and ownership equity are listed as of a specific date, such as the end of its financial year. A _____ is often described as a snapshot of a company's financial condition.

    a. Statement on Auditing Standards No. 70: Service Organizations
    c. Statement of retained earnings
    b. Financial statements
    d. Balance sheet

12. In business and accounting, _____s are everything of value that is owned by a person or company. The balance sheet of a firm records the monetary value of the _____s owned by the firm. The two major _____ classes are tangible _____s and intangible _____s.

    a. Asset
    c. Income
    b. Accounts payable
    d. EBITDA

13. In the United States, _____ are overnight borrowings by banks to maintain their bank reserves at the Federal Reserve. Banks keep reserves at Federal Reserve Banks to meet their reserve requirements and to clear financial transactions. Transactions in the _____ market enable depository institutions with reserve balances in excess of reserve requirements to lend reserves to institutions with reserve deficiencies.

    a. 4-4-5 Calendar
    c. Regulation T
    b. Federal funds rate
    d. Federal funds

14. In the United States, the _____ is the interest rate at which private depository institutions (mostly banks) lend balances (federal funds) at the Federal Reserve to other depository institutions, usually overnight. Changing the target rate is one form of open market operations that the Chairman of the Federal Reserve uses to regulate the supply of money in the U.S. economy.

U.S. banks and thrift institutions are obligated by law to maintain certain levels of reserves, either as reserves with the Fed or as vault cash.

    a. Taylor rule
    c. 4-4-5 Calendar
    b. Regulation T
    d. Federal funds rate

Chapter 4. The Federal Reserve System, Monetary Policy, and Interest Rates

15. _____ are the means of implementing monetary policy by which a central bank controls its national money supply by buying and selling government securities, or other financial instruments. Monetary targets, such as interest rates or exchange rates, are used to guide this implementation.

Since most money is now in the form of electronic records, rather than paper records such as banknotes, _____ are conducted simply by electronically increasing or decreasing ('crediting' or 'debiting') the amount of money that a bank has, e.g., in its reserve account at the central bank, in exchange for a bank selling or buying a financial instrument.

a. AAB
b. ABN Amro
c. Open market operations
d. A Random Walk Down Wall Street

16. The _____ is a bank regulation that sets the minimum reserves each bank must hold to customer deposits and notes. These reserves are designed to satisfy withdrawal demands, and would normally be in the form of fiat currency stored in a bank vault (vault cash), or with a central bank.

The reserve ratio is sometimes used as a tool in the monetary policy, influencing the country's economy, borrowing, and interest rates.

a. Variable rate mortgage
b. Wall Street Journal prime rate
c. Prime rate
d. Reserve requirement

17. _____ is the provision of resources (such as granting a loan) by one party to another party where that second party does not reimburse the first party immediately, thereby generating a debt, and instead arranges either to repay or return those resources (or material(s) of equal value) at a later date. The first party is called a creditor, also known as a lender, while the second party is called a debtor, also known as a borrower.

Movements of financial capital are normally dependent on either _____ or equity transfers.

a. Warrant
b. Clearing house
c. Comparable
d. Credit

18. In economics, the _____ is the proposition by Irving Fisher that the real interest rate is independent of monetary measures, especially the nominal interest rate. The Fisher equation is

$r_r = r_n >- >\pi^e$.

This means, the real interest rate (r_r) equals the nominal interest rate (r_n) minus expected rate of inflation ($>\pi^e$.) Here all the rates are continuously compounded.

a. Fisher hypothesis
b. 7-Eleven
c. 529 plan
d. 4-4-5 Calendar

19. _____ is a fee paid on borrowed assets. It is the price paid for the use of borrowed money, or, money earned by deposited funds. Assets that are sometimes lent with _____ include money, shares, consumer goods through hire purchase, major assets such as aircraft, and even entire factories in finance lease arrangements.
   a. Insolvency
   b. A Random Walk Down Wall Street
   c. AAB
   d. Interest

20. An _____ is the price a borrower pays for the use of money they do not own, and the return a lender receives for deferring the use of funds, by lending it to the borrower. _____s are normally expressed as a percentage rate over the period of one year.

   _____s targets are also a vital tool of monetary policy and are used to control variables like investment, inflation, and unemployment.

   a. AAB
   b. Interest rate
   c. ABN Amro
   d. A Random Walk Down Wall Street

21. In economics, _____ is the total amount of money available in an economy at a particular point in time. There are several ways to define 'money', but each includes currency in circulation and demand deposits.

   _____ data are recorded and published.

   a. 529 plan
   b. 7-Eleven
   c. Money supply
   d. 4-4-5 Calendar

Chapter 5. Money Markets

1. In finance, the _____ is the global financial market for short-term borrowing and lending. It provides short-term liquidity funding for the global financial system. The _____ is where short-term obligations such as Treasury bills, commercial paper and bankers' acceptances are bought and sold.
    - a. Consumer debt
    - b. Cramdown
    - c. Debt-for-equity swap
    - d. Money market

2. A _____ is a fungible, negotiable instrument representing financial value. They are broadly categorized into debt securities (such as banknotes, bonds and debentures), and equity securities; e.g., common stocks. The company or other entity issuing the _____ is called the issuer.
    - a. Tracking stock
    - b. Securities lending
    - c. Security
    - d. Book entry

3. In finance, a _____ is a debt security, in which the authorized issuer owes the holders a debt and, depending on the terms of the _____, is obliged to pay interest (the coupon) and/or to repay the principal at a later date, termed maturity.

    Thus a _____ is a loan: the issuer is the borrower, the _____ holder is the lender, and the coupon is the interest. _____s provide the borrower with external funds to finance long-term investments, or, in the case of government _____s, to finance current expenditure.

    - a. Puttable bond
    - b. Catastrophe bonds
    - c. Bond
    - d. Convertible bond

4. The _____ is a financial market where participants buy and sell debt securities, usually in the form of bonds. As of 2006, the size of the international _____ is an estimated $45 trillion, of which the size of the outstanding U.S. _____ debt was $25.2 trillion.

    Nearly all of the $923 billion average daily trading volume in the U.S. _____ takes place between broker-dealers and large institutions in a decentralized, over-the-counter market.

    - a. 4-4-5 Calendar
    - b. 529 plan
    - c. Fixed income
    - d. Bond market

5. In finance, _____ occurs when a debtor has not met its legal obligations according to the debt contract, e.g. it has not made a scheduled payment, or has violated a loan covenant (condition) of the debt contract. _____ may occur if the debtor is either unwilling or unable to pay their debt. This can occur with all debt obligations including bonds, mortgages, loans, and promissory notes.
    - a. Debt validation
    - b. Default
    - c. Vendor finance
    - d. Credit crunch

6. _____ is the risk of loss due to a debtor's non-payment of a loan or other line of credit (either the principal or interest (coupon) or both)

Most lenders employ their own models (credit scorecards) to rank potential and existing customers according to risk, and then apply appropriate strategies. With products such as unsecured personal loans or mortgages, lenders charge a higher price for higher risk customers and vice versa. With revolving products such as credit cards and overdrafts, risk is controlled through careful setting of credit limits.

a. Transaction risk
b. Liquidity risk
c. Market risk
d. Credit risk

7. _____ or economic opportunity loss is the value of the next best alternative foregone as the result of making a decision. _____ analysis is an important part of a company's decision-making processes but is not treated as an actual cost in any financial statement. The next best thing that a person can engage in is referred to as the _____ of doing the best thing and ignoring the next best thing to be done.
   a. A Random Walk Down Wall Street
   b. AAB
   c. Opportunity cost
   d. ABN Amro

8. _____ is the discipline of identifying, monitoring and limiting risks. In some cases the acceptable risk may be near zero. Risks can come from accidents, natural causes and disasters as well as deliberate attacks from an adversary.
   a. FIFO
   b. Penny stock
   c. 4-4-5 Calendar
   d. Risk management

9. In economics, business, and accounting, a _____ is the value of money that has been used up to produce something, and hence is not available for use anymore. In business, the _____ may be one of acquisition, in which case the amount of money expended to acquire it is counted as _____. In this case, money is the input that is gone in order to acquire the thing.
   a. Fixed costs
   b. Cost
   c. Marginal cost
   d. Sliding scale fees

10. A '_____' is a 'Charge' that is paid to obtain the right to delay a payment. Essentially, the payer purchases the right to make a given payment in the future instead of in the Present. The '_____', or 'Charge' that must be paid to delay the payment, is simply the difference between what the payment amount would be if it were paid in the present and what the payment amount would be paid if it were paid in the future.
    a. Value at risk
    b. Risk modeling
    c. Risk aversion
    d. Discount

11. _____ mature in one year or less. Like zero-coupon bonds, they do not pay interest prior to maturity; instead they are sold at a discount of the par value to create a positive yield to maturity. Many regard _____ as the least risky investment available to U.S. investors.
    a. Treasury securities
    b. 4-4-5 Calendar
    c. Treasury Inflation Protected Securities
    d. Treasury bills

12. In finance, the term _____ describes the amount in cash that returns to the owners of a security. Normally it does not include the price variations, at the difference of the total return. _____ applies to various stated rates of return on stocks (common and preferred, and convertible), fixed income instruments (bonds, notes, bills, strips, zero coupon), and some other investment type insurance products (e.g. annuities.)
    a. Yield to maturity
    b. Macaulay duration
    c. 4-4-5 Calendar
    d. Yield

Chapter 5. Money Markets

13. In the global money market, _____ is an unsecured promissory note with a fixed maturity of one to 270 days. _____ is a money-market security issued (sold) by large banks and corporations to get money to meet short term debt obligations (for example, payroll), and is only backed by an issuing bank or corporation's promise to pay the face amount on the maturity date specified on the note. Since it is not backed by collateral, only firms with excellent credit ratings from a recognized rating agency will be able to sell their _____ at a reasonable price.
    a. Commercial paper
    b. Trade-off theory
    c. Book building
    d. Financial distress

14. _____s are deposits denominated in United States dollars at banks outside the United States, and thus are not under the jurisdiction of the Federal Reserve. Consequently, such deposits are subject to much less regulation than similar deposits within the United States, allowing for higher margins. There is nothing 'European' about _____ deposits; a US dollar-denominated deposit in Tokyo or Caracas would likewise be deemed _____ deposits.
    a. AAB
    b. ABN Amro
    c. A Random Walk Down Wall Street
    d. Eurodollar

15. A _____ is a listing of bonds or fixed income instruments and a statistic reflecting the composite value of its components. It is used as a tool to represent the characteristics of its component fixed income instruments. They differ from stock market indices in their complexity.
    a. 7-Eleven
    b. 4-4-5 Calendar
    c. Bond market index
    d. 529 plan

16. The _____ is the financial market where previously issued securities and financial instruments such as stock, bonds, options, and futures are bought and sold. The term '_____' is also used refer to the market for any used goods or assets, or an alternative use for an existing product or asset where the customer base is the second market

    With primary issuances of securities or financial instruments, or the primary market, investors purchase these securities directly from issuers such as corporations issuing shares in an IPO or private placement, or directly from the federal government in the case of treasuries.

    a. Secondary market
    b. Financial market
    c. Delta neutral
    d. Performance attribution

17. In the United States, _____ are overnight borrowings by banks to maintain their bank reserves at the Federal Reserve. Banks keep reserves at Federal Reserve Banks to meet their reserve requirements and to clear financial transactions. Transactions in the _____ market enable depository institutions with reserve balances in excess of reserve requirements to lend reserves to institutions with reserve deficiencies.
    a. Regulation T
    b. 4-4-5 Calendar
    c. Federal funds rate
    d. Federal funds

18. In the United States, the _____ is the interest rate at which private depository institutions (mostly banks) lend balances (federal funds) at the Federal Reserve to other depository institutions, usually overnight. Changing the target rate is one form of open market operations that the Chairman of the Federal Reserve uses to regulate the supply of money in the U.S. economy.

    U.S. banks and thrift institutions are obligated by law to maintain certain levels of reserves, either as reserves with the Fed or as vault cash.

Chapter 5. Money Markets

a. Taylor rule
b. Federal funds rate
c. 4-4-5 Calendar
d. Regulation T

19. A _____ allows a borrower to use a financial security as collateral for a cash loan at a fixed rate of interest. In a repo, the borrower agrees to immediately sell a security to a lender and also agrees to buy the same security from the lender at a fixed price at some later date. A repo is equivalent to a cash transaction combined with a forward contract.
  a. Contango
  b. Total return swap
  c. Volatility arbitrage
  d. Repurchase agreement

20. _____ is the provision of resources (such as granting a loan) by one party to another party where that second party does not reimburse the first party immediately, thereby generating a debt, and instead arranges either to repay or return those resources (or material(s) of equal value) at a later date. The first party is called a creditor, also known as a lender, while the second party is called a debtor, also known as a borrower.

Movements of financial capital are normally dependent on either _____ or equity transfers.

  a. Credit
  b. Clearing house
  c. Warrant
  d. Comparable

21. A _____ assesses the credit worthiness of an individual, corporation, or even a country. _____s are calculated from financial history and current assets and liabilities. Typically, a _____ tells a lender or investor the probability of the subject being able to pay back a loan.
  a. Credit cycle
  b. Debenture
  c. Credit report monitoring
  d. Credit rating

22. A _____ is a document that indicates that the bearer of the document has title to property, such as shares or bonds. They differ from normal registered instruments, in that no records are kept of who owns the underlying property, or of the transactions involving transfer of ownership. Whoever physically holds the bearer bond papers owns the property.
  a. Book entry
  b. Bearer instrument
  c. Marketable
  d. Securities lending

23. A _____ s a time deposit, a financial product commonly offered to consumers by banks, thrift institutions, and credit unions.

They are similar to savings accounts in that they are insured and thus virtually risk-free; they are 'money in the bank'. They are different from savings accounts in that they have a specific, fixed term (often three months, six months, or one to five years), and, usually, a fixed interest rate.

  a. Reserve requirement
  b. Certificate of deposit
  c. Variable rate mortgage
  d. Time deposit

24. The _____ , a component of the Federal Reserve System, is charged under United States law with overseeing the nation's open market operations. It is the Federal Reserve Committee that makes key decisions about interest rates and the growth jam of the United States money supply. It is the principal organ of United States national monetary policy.

Chapter 5. Money Markets

a. Fiscal policy
b. Tax incidence
c. Tax exemption
d. Federal Open Market Committee

25. _____ is the process by which the government, or monetary authority of a country controls (i) the supply of money central bank (ii) availability of money, and (iii) cost of money or rate of interest, in order to attain a set of objectives oriented towards the growth and stability of the economy. Monetary theory provides insight into how to craft optimal _____.

_____ is referred to as either being an expansionary policy where an expansionary policy increases the total supply of money in the economy, and a contractionary policy decreases the total money supply.

a. Natural resources consumption tax
b. Federal Open Market Committee
c. Monetary policy
d. Tax exemption

26. The institution most often referenced by the word '_____' is a public or publicly traded _____, the shares of which are traded on a public stock exchange (e.g., the New York Stock Exchange or Nasdaq in the United States) where shares of stock of _____s are bought and sold by and to the general public. Most of the largest businesses in the world are publicly traded _____s. However, the majority of _____s are said to be closely held, privately held or close _____s, meaning that no ready market exists for the trading of shares.

a. Depository Trust Company
b. Protect
c. Federal Home Loan Mortgage Corporation
d. Corporation

27. The _____ (LIBID) is a bid rate; the rate bid by banks on Eurocurrency deposits (i.e., the rate at which a bank is willing to borrow from other banks.) It is 'the opposite' of the LIBOR (an offered, hence 'ask' rate.) Whilst the British Bankers' Association set LIBOR rates, there is no correspondent official LIBID fixing.

a. Cash accumulation equation
b. Shanghai Interbank Offered Rate
c. Repo rate
d. London Interbank Bid Rate

28. The _____ is a daily reference rate based on the interest rates at which banks borrow unsecured funds from banks in the London wholesale money market (or interbank market.) It is roughly comparable to the U.S. Federal funds rate.

During 1984 it became apparent that an increasing number of banks were trading actively in a variety of relatively new market instruments, notably interest rate swaps, foreign currency options and forward rate agreements.

a. Shanghai Interbank Offered Rate
b. Fixed interest
c. London Interbank Offered Rate
d. Risk-free interest rate

Chapter 6. Bond Markets

1. In finance, a _____ is a debt security, in which the authorized issuer owes the holders a debt and, depending on the terms of the _____, is obliged to pay interest (the coupon) and/or to repay the principal at a later date, termed maturity.

Thus a _____ is a loan: the issuer is the borrower, the _____ holder is the lender, and the coupon is the interest. _____s provide the borrower with external funds to finance long-term investments, or, in the case of government _____s, to finance current expenditure.

   a. Catastrophe bonds
   c. Convertible bond
   b. Puttable bond
   d. Bond

2. The _____ is a financial market where participants buy and sell debt securities, usually in the form of bonds. As of 2006, the size of the international _____ is an estimated $45 trillion, of which the size of the outstanding U.S. _____ debt was $25.2 trillion.

Nearly all of the $923 billion average daily trading volume in the U.S. _____ takes place between broker-dealers and large institutions in a decentralized, over-the-counter market.

   a. Bond market
   c. Fixed income
   b. 4-4-5 Calendar
   d. 529 plan

3. _____ are dollar-denominated bonds, issued mostly by Latin American countries in the 1980s, named after U.S. Treasury Secretary Nicholas Brady.

_____ were created in March 1989 in order to convert bonds issued by mostly Latin American countries into a variety or 'menu' of new bonds after many of those countries defaulted on their debt in the 1980's. At that time, the market for sovereign debt was small and illiquid, and the standardization of emerging-market debt facilitated risk-spreading and trading.

   a. Coupon rate
   c. Brady bonds
   b. Nominal yield
   d. Municipal bond

4. The _____ is the market for securities, where companies and governments can raise longterm funds. The _____ includes the stock market and the bond market. Financial regulators, such as the U.S. Securities and Exchange Commission, oversee the _____s in their designated countries to ensure that investors are protected against fraud.
   a. Spot rate
   c. Forward market
   b. Delta neutral
   d. Capital market

5. A _____ is a fungible, negotiable instrument representing financial value. They are broadly categorized into debt securities (such as banknotes, bonds and debentures), and equity securities; e.g., common stocks. The company or other entity issuing the _____ is called the issuer.
   a. Book entry
   c. Securities lending
   b. Tracking stock
   d. Security

Chapter 6. Bond Markets

6. _____ are government bonds issued by the United States Department of the Treasury through the Bureau of the Public Debt. They are the debt financing instruments of the U.S. Federal government, and they are often referred to simply as Treasuries or Treasurys. There are four types of marketable _____: Treasury bills, Treasury notes, Treasury bonds, and Treasury Inflation Protected Securities (TIPS.)

   a. Treasury Inflation Protected Securities   b. Treasury Inflation-Protected Securities
   c. Treasury securities   d. 4-4-5 Calendar

7. _____ is that which is owed; usually referencing assets owed, but the term can cover other obligations. In the case of assets, _____ is a means of using future purchasing power in the present before a summation has been earned. Some companies and corporations use _____ as a part of their overall corporate finance strategy.

   a. Partial Payment   b. Credit cycle
   c. Cross-collateralization   d. Debt

8. In finance, _____ is the interest that has accumulated since the principal investment, or since the previous interest payment if there has been one already. For a financial instrument such as a bond, interest is calculated and paid in set intervals.

The primary formula for calculating the interest accrued in a given period is:

$$I_A = T \times P \times R$$

where I_A is the _____, T is the fraction of the year, P is the principal, and R is the annualized interest rate.

   a. AAB   b. ABN Amro
   c. A Random Walk Down Wall Street   d. Accrued interest

9. In finance, the _____ is the price of a bond excluding any interest that has accrued since issue or the most recent coupon payment. This is to be compared with the dirty price, which is the price of a bond including the accrued interest.

When bond prices are quoted on a Bloomberg Terminal or Reuters they are quoted using the _____.

   a. Clean price   b. Gilts
   c. Bond valuation   d. Bowie bonds

10. The _____ of a bond represents the value of a bond, exclusive of any commissions or fees. The _____ is also called the 'full price.'

Bonds, as well as a variety of other fixed income securities, provide for coupon payments to be made to bond holders on a fixed schedule. The _____ of a bond will decrease on the days coupons are paid, resulting in a saw-tooth pattern for the bond value.

   a. Collateralized debt obligations   b. Premium bond
   c. Dirty price   d. Serial bond

Chapter 6. Bond Markets

11. _____ are the inflation-indexed bonds issued by the U.S. Treasury. The principal is adjusted to the Consumer Price Index, the commonly used measure of inflation. The coupon rate is constant, but generates a different amount of interest when multiplied by the inflation-adjusted principal, thus protecting the holder against inflation. _____ are currently offered in 5-year, 10-year and 20-year maturities.
   a. 4-4-5 Calendar
   b. Treasury securities
   c. Treasury Inflation-Protected Securities
   d. Treasury Inflation Protected Securities

12. _____ is a fee paid on borrowed assets. It is the price paid for the use of borrowed money, or, money earned by deposited funds. Assets that are sometimes lent with _____ include money, shares, consumer goods through hire purchase, major assets such as aircraft, and even entire factories in finance lease arrangements.
   a. AAB
   b. A Random Walk Down Wall Street
   c. Interest
   d. Insolvency

13. In finance, the term _____ describes the amount in cash that returns to the owners of a security. Normally it does not include the price variations, at the difference of the total return. _____ applies to various stated rates of return on stocks (common and preferred, and convertible), fixed income instruments (bonds, notes, bills, strips, zero coupon), and some other investment type insurance products (e.g. annuities.)
   a. Macaulay duration
   b. 4-4-5 Calendar
   c. Yield to maturity
   d. Yield

14. The _____ or redemption yield is the yield promised to the bondholder on the assumption that the bond or other fixed-interest security such as gilts will be held to maturity, that all coupon and principal payments will be made and coupon payments are reinvested at the bond's promised yield at the same rate as invested. It is a measure of the return of the bond. This technique in theory allows investors to calculate the fair value of different financial instruments.
   a. Yield to maturity
   b. Yield
   c. Macaulay duration
   d. 4-4-5 Calendar

15. In economics, _____ is a rise in the general level of prices of goods and services in an economy over a period of time. The term '_____' once referred to increases in the money supply (monetary _____); however, economic debates about the relationship between money supply and price levels have led to its primary use today in describing price _____. _____ can also be described as a decline in the real value of money--a loss of purchasing power in the medium of exchange which is also the monetary unit of account.
   a. AAB
   b. ABN Amro
   c. A Random Walk Down Wall Street
   d. Inflation

16. _____ is a life of security. It may also refer to the final payment date of a loan or other financial instrument, at which point all remaining interest and principal is due to be paid.

1, 3, 6 months _____ band can be calculated by using 30-day per month periods.

   a. Maturity
   b. False billing
   c. Primary market
   d. Replacement cost

17. A _____ is an international bond that is denominated in a currency not native to the country where it is issued. It can be categorised according to the currency in which it is issued. London is one of the centers of the _____ market, but _____s may be traded throughout the world - for example in Singapore or Tokyo.

Chapter 6. Bond Markets

a. Eurobond
b. Economic entity
c. Interest rate option
d. Education production function

18. In the United States, a _____ is a bond issued by a city or other local government, or their agencies. Potential issuers of these bonds include cities, counties, redevelopment agencies, school districts, publicly owned airports and seaports, and any other governmental entity (or group of governments) below the state level. They may be general obligations of the issuer or secured by specified revenues.
   a. Senior debt
   b. Puttable bond
   c. Municipal bond
   d. Premium bond

19. In the global money market, _____ is an unsecured promissory note with a fixed maturity of one to 270 days. _____ is a money-market security issued (sold) by large banks and corporations to get money to meet short term debt obligations (for example, payroll), and is only backed by an issuing bank or corporation's promise to pay the face amount on the maturity date specified on the note. Since it is not backed by collateral, only firms with excellent credit ratings from a recognized rating agency will be able to sell their _____ at a reasonable price.
   a. Book building
   b. Trade-off theory
   c. Financial distress
   d. Commercial paper

20. The _____ is the financial market where previously issued securities and financial instruments such as stock, bonds, options, and futures are bought and sold. The term '_____' is also used refer to the market for any used goods or assets, or an alternative use for an existing product or asset where the customer base is the second market

With primary issuances of securities or financial instruments, or the primary market, investors purchase these securities directly from issuers such as corporations issuing shares in an IPO or private placement, or directly from the federal government in the case of treasuries.

   a. Financial market
   b. Performance attribution
   c. Delta neutral
   d. Secondary market

21. A _____ is a legal pledge in United States municipal finance, in which an entity pledges its full faith and credit to repay its debt, typically a _____ bond.
   a. Covenant
   b. Financial Institutions Reform Recovery and Enforcement Act
   c. Letter of credit
   d. General obligation

22. A _____ is a listing of bonds or fixed income instruments and a statistic reflecting the composite value of its components. It is used as a tool to represent the characteristics of its component fixed income instruments. They differ from stock market indices in their complexity.
   a. 7-Eleven
   b. 529 plan
   c. 4-4-5 Calendar
   d. Bond market index

23. In business, _____ is income that a company receives from its normal business activities, usually from the sale of goods and services to customers. Some companies also receive _____ from interest, dividends or royalties paid to them by other companies. _____ may refer to business income in general, or it may refer to the amount, in a monetary unit, received during a period of time, as in 'Last year, Company X had _____ of $32 million.'

In many countries, including the UK, _____ is referred to as turnover.

a. Furniture, Fixtures and Equipment
b. Matching principle
c. Bottom line
d. Revenue

24. _____ are bonds issued by governments, authorities, or public benefit corporations that are guaranteed by the revenue flow of the issuing agency.

The Supreme Court decision of Pollock versus Farmer's Loan and Trust Company of 1895 initiated a wave or series of innovations for the financial services community in both tax-treatment and regulation from government. This specific case, according to a leading investment bank's research, resulted in the 'intergovernmental tax immunity doctrine,' ultimately leading to 'tax-free status.' Municipal bonds are generally exempt from federal tax on their interest payments (not capital gains.)

a. Private activity bond
b. Gilts
c. Callable bond
d. Revenue bonds

25. In the _____ contract the underwriter guarantees the sale of the issued stock at the agreed-upon price. For the issuer, it is the safest but the most expensive type of the contracts, since the underwriter takes the risk of sale.

In the best efforts contract the underwriter agrees to sell as many shares as possible at the agreed-upon price.

a. Firm commitment
b. Special purpose entity
c. Participating preferred stock
d. Rights issue

26. Unemployment occurs when a person is available to work and currently seeking work, but the person is without work. The prevalence of unemployment is usually measured using the _____, which is defined as the percentage of those in the labor force who are unemployed. The _____ is also used in economic studies and economic indexes such as the United States' Conference Board's Index of Leading Indicators as a measure of the state of the macroeconomics.

a. A Random Walk Down Wall Street
b. ABN Amro
c. AAB
d. Unemployment rate

27. In the United States, a _____ is an offering of securities that are not registered with the Securities and Exchange Commission (SEC.) Such offerings exploit an exemption offered by the Securities Act of 1933 that comes with several restrictions, including a prohibition against general solicitation. This exemption allows companies to avoid quarterly reporting requirements and many of the legal liabilities associated with the Sarbanes-Oxley Act.

a. 529 plan
b. 7-Eleven
c. 4-4-5 Calendar
d. Private placement

28. A _____ is a document that indicates that the bearer of the document has title to property, such as shares or bonds. They differ from normal registered instruments, in that no records are kept of who owns the underlying property, or of the transactions involving transfer of ownership. Whoever physically holds the bearer bond papers owns the property.

a. Book entry
b. Marketable
c. Securities lending
d. Bearer instrument

Chapter 6. Bond Markets

29. A _____ is different from normal stock in that it is unregistered - no records are kept of the owner, or the transactions involving ownership. Whoever physically holds the _____ papers owns the stock or corporation. This is useful for investors and corporate officers who wish to retain anonymity.
   a. Clean price
   b. Gilts
   c. Revenue bonds
   d. Bearer bond

30. _____ (also trust indenture or deed of trust) is a legal document issued to lenders and describes key terms such as the interest rate, maturity date, convertibility, pledge, promises, representations, covenants, and other terms of the bond offering. When the Offering Memorandum is prepared in advance of marketing a Bond, the indenture will typically be summarised in the 'Description of Notes' section.
   a. McFadden Act
   b. Fair Labor Standards Act
   c. Court of Audit of Belgium
   d. Bond indenture

31. A _____ is a bond issued by a corporation. The term is usually applied to longer-term debt instruments, generally with a maturity date falling at least a year after their issue date. (The term 'commercial paper' is sometimes used for instruments with a shorter maturity.)
   a. Corporate bond
   b. Brady bonds
   c. Government bond
   d. Serial bond

32. In finance, a _____ is a type of bond that can be converted into shares of stock in the issuing company, usually at some pre-announced ratio. It is a hybrid security with debt- and equity-like features. Although it typically has a low coupon rate, the holder is compensated with the ability to convert the bond to common stock, usually at a substantial discount to the stock's market value.
   a. Corporate bond
   b. Gilts
   c. Bond fund
   d. Convertible bond

33. A _____ is defined as a certificate of agreement of loans which is given under the company's stamp and carries an undertaking that the _____ holder will get a fixed return (fixed on the basis of interest rates) and the principal amount whenever the _____ matures.

In finance, a _____ is a long-term debt instrument used by governments and large companies to obtain funds. It is defined as 'a debt secured only by the debtor's earning power, not by a lien on any specific asset.' It is similar to a bond except the securitization conditions are different.

   a. Collateral Management
   b. Partial Payment
   c. Collection agency
   d. Debenture

34. _____s are financial bonds that mature in installments over a period of time. In effect, a $100,000, 5-year _____ would mature in a $20,000 annuity over a 5-year interval. Bond issues consisting of a series of blocks of securities maturing in sequence, the coupon rate can be different.
   a. Serial bond
   b. Brady bonds
   c. Callable bond
   d. Bond fund

Chapter 6. Bond Markets

35. _____ is a type of bond that allows the issuer of the bond to retain the privilege of redeeming the bond at some point before the bond reaches the date of maturity. In other words, on the call dates, the issuer has the right, but not the obligation, to buy back the bonds from the bond holders at the call price. Technically speaking, the bonds are not really bought and held by the issuer but cancelled immediately.
   a. Gilts
   b. Coupon rate
   c. Bond fund
   d. Callable bond

36. In financial accounting, _____s are precautions for which the amount or probability of occurrence are not known. Typical examples are _____s for warranty costs and _____ for taxes the term reserve is used instead of term _____; such a use, however, is inconsistent with the terminology suggested by International Accounting Standards Board.
   a. Provision
   b. Money measurement concept
   c. Petty cash
   d. Momentum Accounting and Triple-Entry Bookkeeping

37. In finance, a _____ is a security that entitles the holder to buy stock of the company that issued it at a specified price, which is usually higher than the stock price at time of issue.

_____s are frequently attached to bonds or preferred stock as a sweetener, allowing the issuer to pay lower interest rates or dividends. They can be used to enhance the yield of the bond, and make them more attractive to potential buyers.

   a. Warrant
   b. Credit
   c. Clearing
   d. Clearing house

38. _____ refers to any type of investment that yields a regular (or fixed) return.

For example, if you lend money to a borrower and the borrower has to pay interest once a month, you have been issued a fixed-income security. When a company does this, it is often called a bond or corporate bank debt (although preferred stock is also sometimes considered to be _____).

   a. 4-4-5 Calendar
   b. Bond market
   c. 529 plan
   d. Fixed Income

39. _____, refers to consumption opportunity gained by an entity within a specified time frame, which is generally expressed in monetary terms. However, for households and individuals, '_____ is the sum of all the wages, salaries, profits, interests payments, rents and other forms of earnings received... in a given period of time.' For firms, _____ generally refers to net-profit: what remains of revenue after expenses have been subtracted.
   a. Accrual
   b. OIBDA
   c. Income
   d. Annual report

40. The _____ is a stock exchange based in New York City, New York. It is the largest stock exchange in the world by dollar value of its listed companies securities. As of October 2008, the combined capitalization of all domestic _____ listed companies was $10.1 trillion.

Chapter 6. Bond Markets

a. 4-4-5 Calendar
c. 7-Eleven
b. 529 plan
d. New York Stock Exchange

41. A _____ is a fund established by a government agency or business for the purpose of reducing debt.

The _____ was first used in Great Britain in the 18th century to reduce national debt. While used by Robert Walpole in 1716 and effectively in the 1720s and early 1730s, it originated in the commercial tax syndicates of the Italian peninsula of the 14th century to retire redeemable public debt of those cities.

a. Security interest
c. Modern portfolio theory
b. Debtor
d. Sinking fund

42. A _____, securities exchange or (in Europe) bourse is a corporation or mutual organization which provides 'trading' facilities for stock brokers and traders, to trade stocks and other securities. _____s also provide facilities for the issue and redemption of securities as well as other financial instruments and capital events including the payment of income and dividends. The securities traded on a _____ include: shares issued by companies, unit trusts and other pooled investment products and bonds.

a. 7-Eleven
c. 529 plan
b. 4-4-5 Calendar
d. Stock Exchange

43. _____ is the provision of resources (such as granting a loan) by one party to another party where that second party does not reimburse the first party immediately, thereby generating a debt, and instead arranges either to repay or return those resources (or material(s) of equal value) at a later date. The first party is called a creditor, also known as a lender, while the second party is called a debtor, also known as a borrower.

Movements of financial capital are normally dependent on either _____ or equity transfers.

a. Clearing house
c. Comparable
b. Warrant
d. Credit

44. A _____ assesses the credit worthiness of an individual, corporation, or even a country. _____s are calculated from financial history and current assets and liabilities. Typically, a _____ tells a lender or investor the probability of the subject being able to pay back a loan.

a. Credit rating
c. Credit report monitoring
b. Debenture
d. Credit cycle

45. In finance, _____ occurs when a debtor has not met its legal obligations according to the debt contract, e.g. it has not made a scheduled payment, or has violated a loan covenant (condition) of the debt contract. _____ may occur if the debtor is either unwilling or unable to pay their debt. This can occur with all debt obligations including bonds, mortgages, loans, and promissory notes.

a. Default
c. Debt validation
b. Vendor finance
d. Credit crunch

46. In finance, a _____ (non-investment grade bond, speculative grade bond or junk bond) is a bond that is rated below investment grade at the time of purchase. These bonds have a higher risk of default or other adverse credit events, but typically pay higher yields than better quality bonds in order to make them attractive to investors.

a. Private equity
b. High yield bond
c. Sharpe ratio
d. Volatility

47. In finance, a _____ is a derivative in which two counterparties agree to exchange one stream of cash flows against another stream. These streams are called the legs of the _____.

The cash flows are calculated over a notional principal amount, which is usually not exchanged between counterparties.

a. Volatility swap
b. Swap
c. Local volatility
d. Volatility arbitrage

Chapter 7. Mortgage Markets

1. A _____ is a fungible, negotiable instrument representing financial value. They are broadly categorized into debt securities (such as banknotes, bonds and debentures), and equity securities; e.g., common stocks. The company or other entity issuing the _____ is called the issuer.
   a. Book entry
   b. Securities lending
   c. Security
   d. Tracking stock

2. In finance, a _____ is a debt security, in which the authorized issuer owes the holders a debt and, depending on the terms of the _____, is obliged to pay interest (the coupon) and/or to repay the principal at a later date, termed maturity.

   Thus a _____ is a loan: the issuer is the borrower, the _____ holder is the lender, and the coupon is the interest. _____s provide the borrower with external funds to finance long-term investments, or, in the case of government _____s, to finance current expenditure.

   a. Catastrophe bonds
   b. Puttable bond
   c. Convertible bond
   d. Bond

3. The _____ is a financial market where participants buy and sell debt securities, usually in the form of bonds. As of 2006, the size of the international _____ is an estimated $45 trillion, of which the size of the outstanding U.S. _____ debt was $25.2 trillion.

   Nearly all of the $923 billion average daily trading volume in the U.S. _____ takes place between broker-dealers and large institutions in a decentralized, over-the-counter market.

   a. 529 plan
   b. 4-4-5 Calendar
   c. Fixed income
   d. Bond market

4. In lending agreements, _____ is a borrower's pledge of specific property to a lender, to secure repayment of a loan. The _____ serves as protection for a lender against a borrower's risk of default - that is, a borrower failing to pay the principal and interest under the terms of a loan obligation. If a borrower does default on a loan (due to insolvency or other event), that borrower forfeits (gives up) the property pledged as _____ *ollateral* - and the lender then becomes the owner of the _____.
   a. Nominal value
   b. Future-oriented
   c. Refinancing risk
   d. Collateral

5. A _____ is a loan made using real estate as collateral to secure repayment.

   A _____ is similar to a residential mortgage, except the collateral is a commercial building or other business real estate, not residential property.

   In addition, _____s are typically taken on by businesses instead of individual borrowers.

   a. Chain of Blame
   b. Shared appreciation mortgage
   c. Commercial mortgage
   d. Fixed rate mortgage

Chapter 7. Mortgage Markets

6. _____ is a term used in the context of the purchase of expensive items such as a car and a house, whereby the payment is the initial upfront portion of the total amount due and it is usually given in cash at the time of finalizing the transaction. A loan is then required to make the full payment.

The main purpose of a _____ is to ensure that the lending institution can recover the balance due on the loan in the event that the borrower defaults.

a. Royalties

b. Financial Institutions Reform Recovery and Enforcement Act

c. Business valuation

d. Down payment

7. The _____ is a federally chartered network of borrower-owned lending institutions composed of cooperatives and related service organizations. Cooperatives are organizations that are owned and controlled by their members who use the cooperative'e;s products, supplies or services. The U.S. Congress authorized the creation of the first System institutions in 1916.

a. 4-4-5 Calendar

b. 529 plan

c. 7-Eleven

d. Farm credit system

8. In law, a _____ is a form of security interest granted over an item of property to secure the payment of a debt or performance of some other obligation. The owner of the property, who grants the _____, is referred to as the lienor and the person who has the benefit of the _____ is referred to as the _____ee.

The etymological root is: Anglo-French _____, loyen bond, restraint, from Latin ligamen, from ligare to bind.

a. Joint venture

b. Family and Medical Leave Act

c. Sarbanes-Oxley Act

d. Lien

9. _____ is the provision of resources (such as granting a loan) by one party to another party where that second party does not reimburse the first party immediately, thereby generating a debt, and instead arranges either to repay or return those resources (or material(s) of equal value) at a later date. The first party is called a creditor, also known as a lender, while the second party is called a debtor, also known as a borrower.

Movements of financial capital are normally dependent on either _____ or equity transfers.

a. Credit

b. Warrant

c. Comparable

d. Clearing house

10. The _____ is that part of the capital markets that deals with the issuance of new securities. Companies, governments or public sector institutions can obtain funding through the sale of a new stock or bond issue. This is typically done through a syndicate of securities dealers.

a. Volatility clustering

b. Peer group analysis

c. Sector rotation

d. Primary market

Chapter 7. Mortgage Markets

11. _____ is insurance payable to a lender or trustee for a pool of securities that may be required when taking out a mortgage loan. It is insurance to offset losses in the case where a mortgagor is not able to repay the loan and the lender is not able to recover its costs after foreclosure and sale of the mortgaged property. Typical rates are $55/mo. per $100,000 financed, or as high as $1,500/yr. for a typical $200,000 loan.
    a. 4-4-5 Calendar
    b. Lenders Mortgage Insurance
    c. 529 plan
    d. Property insurance

12. _____ is an insurance policy which compensates lenders or investors for losses due to the default of a mortgage loan. _____ can be either public or private depending upon the insurer. The policy is also known as a mortgage indemnity guarantee (Mortgage insuranceG), particularly in the UK.
    a. Reverse mortgage
    b. Subprime lending
    c. Mortgage-backed security
    d. Mortgage insurance

13. _____ is the process of decreasing an amount over a period of time. The word comes from Middle English amortisen to kill, alienate in mortmain, from Anglo-French amorteser, alteration of amortir, from Vulgar Latin admortire to kill, from Latin ad- + mort-, mors death. Particular instances of the term include:

    - _____ (business), the allocation of a lump sum amount to different time periods, particularly for loans and other forms of finance, including related interest or other finance charges.
        o _____ schedule, a table detailing each periodic payment on a loan (typically a mortgage), as generated by an _____ calculator.
        o Negative _____, an _____ schedule where the loan amount actually increases through not paying the full interest
    - Amortized analysis, analyzing the execution cost of algorithms over a sequence of operations.
    - _____ of capital expenditures of certain assets under accounting rules, particularly intangible assets, in a manner analogous to depreciation.
    - _____ (tax law)

_____ is also used in the context of zoning regulations and describes the time in which a property owner has to relocate when the property's use constitutes a preexisting nonconforming use under zoning regulations.

    - Depreciation

    a. Option
    b. Intrinsic value
    c. AT'T Inc.
    d. Amortization

14. The phrase _____ or bullet payment refers to one of two ways for repaying a loan; the other type is called amortizing payment or Amortization (business).

With a balloon loan, a _____ is paid back when the loan comes to its contractual maturity, e.g. reaches the deadline set to repayment at the time the loan was granted, representing the full loan amount (also called principal.) Periodic interest payments are generally made throughout the life of the loan.

Chapter 7. Mortgage Markets

a. Present value of costs
b. Future-oriented
c. Refinancing risk
d. Balloon payment

15. A _____ is a mortgage which does not fully amortize over the term of the note, thus leaving a balance due at maturity. The final payment is called a balloon payment because of its large size. _____s are more common in commercial real estate than in residential real estate.
a. Balloon payment mortgage
b. Chain of Blame
c. HELOC
d. Negative equity

16. The _____ duty is a legal relationship of confidence or trust between two or more parties, most commonly a _____ or trustee and a principal or beneficiary. One party, for example a corporate trust company or the trust department of a bank, holds a _____ relation or acts in a _____ capacity to another, such as one whose funds are entrusted to it for investment. In a _____ relation one person justifiably reposes confidence, good faith, reliance and trust in another whose aid, advice or protection is sought in some matter.
a. General obligation
b. Legal tender
c. Financial Institutions Reform Recovery and Enforcement Act
d. Fiduciary

17. An _____ is a mortgage loan where the interest rate on the note is periodically adjusted based on a variety of indices. Among the most common indices are the rates on 1-year constant-maturity Treasury (CMT) securities, the Cost of Funds Index (COFI), and the London Interbank Offered Rate (LIBOR.) A few lenders use their own cost of funds as an index, rather than using other indices.
a. A Random Walk Down Wall Street
b. ABN Amro
c. AAB
d. Adjustable rate mortgage

18. A '_____' is a 'Charge' that is paid to obtain the right to delay a payment. Essentially, the payer purchases the right to make a given payment in the future instead of in the Present. The '_____', or 'Charge' that must be paid to delay the payment, is simply the difference between what the payment amount would be if it were paid in the present and what the payment amount would be paid if it were paid in the future.
a. Risk modeling
b. Discount
c. Risk aversion
d. Value at risk

19. _____ in the United States is indemnity insurance against financial loss from defects in title to real property and from the invalidity or unenforceability of mortgage liens. _____ is principally a product developed and sold in the United States as a result of the comparative deficiency of the US land records laws. It is meant to protect an owner's or a lender's financial interest in real property against loss due to title defects, liens or other matters.
a. 529 plan
b. Preferred provider organization
c. 4-4-5 Calendar
d. Title insurance

20. _____ refers to the replacement of an existing debt obligation with a debt obligation bearing different terms. The most common consumer _____ is for a home mortgage.

_____ may be undertaken to reduce interest rate/interest costs (by _____ at a lower rate), to extend the repayment time, to pay off other debt(s), to reduce one's periodic payment obligations (sometimes by taking a longer-term loan), to reduce or alter risk (such as by _____ from a variable-rate to a fixed-rate loan), and/or to raise cash for investment, consumption, or the payment of a dividend.

Chapter 7. Mortgage Markets

a. 7-Eleven
c. 4-4-5 Calendar
b. 529 plan
d. Refinancing

21. An _____ is a table detailing each periodic payment on a amortizing loan (typically a mortgage), as generated by an amortization calculator.

While a portion of every payment is applied towards both the interest and the principal balance of the loan, the exact amount applied to principal each time varies (with the remainder going to interest.) An _____ reveals the specific monetary amount put towards interest, as well as the specific put towards the Principal balance, with each payment.

a. Adjusted basis
c. Adjusting entries
b. Amortization schedule
d. Annual report

22. In finance, _____ is the process of estimating the potential market value of a financial asset or liability. they can be done on assets (for example, investments in marketable securities such as stocks, options, business enterprises, or intangible assets such as patents and trademarks) or on liabilities (e.g., Bonds issued by a company.) _____s are required in many contexts including investment analysis, capital budgeting, merger and acquisition transactions, financial reporting, taxable events to determine the proper tax liability, and in litigation.

a. Procter ' Gamble
c. Margin
b. Share
d. Valuation

23. _____ is the value of a homeowner's unencumbered interest in their property, i.e. the difference between the home's fair market value and the unpaid balance of the mortgage and any outstanding debt over the home. _____ increases as the mortgage is paid or as the property enjoys appreciation. This is sometimes called real property value in economics.

a. Real Estate Investment Trust
c. Liquidation value
b. REIT
d. Home equity

24. The _____ is the market for the sale of securities or bonds collateralized by the value of mortgage loans. The mortgage lender, commercial banks, or specialized firm will group together many loans and sell grouped loans as securities called collateralized mortgage obligations (CMOs.) The risk of the individual loans is reduced by that aggregation process.

a. Secondary mortgage market
c. 4-4-5 Calendar
b. 7-Eleven
d. 529 plan

25. The _____ is the financial market where previously issued securities and financial instruments such as stock, bonds, options, and futures are bought and sold. The term '_____' is also used refer to the market for any used goods or assets, or an alternative use for an existing product or asset where the customer base is the second market

With primary issuances of securities or financial instruments, or the primary market, investors purchase these securities directly from issuers such as corporations issuing shares in an IPO or private placement, or directly from the federal government in the case of treasuries.

a. Financial market
c. Performance attribution
b. Delta neutral
d. Secondary market

Chapter 7. Mortgage Markets

26. A _____ is an asset-backed security whose cash flows are backed by the principal and interest payments of a set of mortgage loans. Payments are typically made monthly over the lifetime of the underlying loans.
    a. Home equity line of credit
    b. Conforming loan
    c. Shared appreciation mortgage
    d. Mortgage-backed security

27. In finance, 'participation' is an ownership interest in a mortgage or other loan. In particular, _____ is a cooperation of multiple lenders to issue a loan (known as participation loan) to one borrower. This is usually done in order to reduce individual risks of the lenders.
    a. Loan participation
    b. Short positions
    c. Doctrine of the Proper Law
    d. Securitization

28. The _____ is a U.S. government-owned corporation within the Department of Housing and Urban Development

Ginnie Mae provides guarantees on mortgage-backed securities backed by federally insured or guaranteed loans, mainly loans issued by the Federal Housing Administration, Department of Veterans Affairs, Rural Housing Service, and Office of Public and Indian Housing. Ginnie Mae securities are the only MBS that are guaranteed by the United States government.

    a. GNMA
    b. Cash budget
    c. Case-Shiller Home Price Indices
    d. Certified Emission Reductions

29. The _____ is a U.S. government-owned corporation within the Department of Housing and Urban Development

Ginnie Mae provides guarantees on mortgage-backed securities backed by federally insured or guaranteed loans, mainly loans issued by the Federal Housing Administration, Department of Veterans Affairs, Rural Housing Service, and Office of Public and Indian Housing. Ginnie Mae securities are the only MBS that are guaranteed by the United States government.

    a. 4-4-5 Calendar
    b. Graduated payment mortgage
    c. Government National Mortgage Association
    d. Jumbo mortgage

30. The institution most often referenced by the word '_____' is a public or publicly traded _____, the shares of which are traded on a public stock exchange (e.g., the New York Stock Exchange or Nasdaq in the United States) where shares of stock of _____s are bought and sold by and to the general public. Most of the largest businesses in the world are publicly traded _____s. However, the majority of _____s are said to be closely held, privately held or close _____s, meaning that no ready market exists for the trading of shares.
    a. Federal Home Loan Mortgage Corporation
    b. Depository Trust Company
    c. Protect
    d. Corporation

31. The value of speculative bonds is affected to a higher degree than investment grade bonds by the possibility of default. For example, in a recession interest rates may drop, and the drop in interest rates tends to increase the value of investment grade bonds; however, a recession tends to increase the possibility of default in speculative-grade bonds.

The original speculative grade bonds were bonds that once had been investment grade at time of issue, but where the credit rating of the issuer had slipped and the possibility of default increased significantly. These bonds are called '_____'.

Chapter 7. Mortgage Markets

a. Sharpe ratio
c. Seed round
b. Return on capital employed
d. Fallen angels

32. The _____ (NYSE: FNM), commonly known as Fannie Mae, is a stockholder-owned corporation chartered by Congress in 1968 as a government sponsored enterprise (GSE), but founded in 1938 during the Great Depression. The corporation's purpose is to purchase and securitize mortgages in order to ensure that funds are consistently available to the institutions that lend money to home buyers.

On September 7, 2008, James Lockhart, director of the Federal Housing Finance Agency (FHFA), announced that Fannie Mae and Freddie Mac were being placed into conservatorship of the FHFA.

a. General partnership
c. SPDR
b. The Depository Trust ' Clearing Corporation
d. Federal National Mortgage Association

33. The _____ (NYSE: FRE) is an insolvent government sponsored enterprise (GSE) of the United States federal government.

The _____ was created in 1970 to expand the secondary market for mortgages in the US. Along with other GSEs, Freddie Mac buys mortgages on the secondary market, pools them, and sells them as mortgage-backed securities to investors on the open market.

a. Governmental Accounting Standards Board
c. The Depository Trust ' Clearing Corporation
b. Public company
d. Federal Home Loan Mortgage Corporation

34. The _____ provide stable, on-demand, low-cost funding to American financial institutions for home mortgage loans, small business, rural, agricultural, and economic development lending. With their members, the _____ank System represents the largest collective source of home mortgage and community credit in the United States. The banks do not provide loans directly to individuals, only to other banks.

a. 4-4-5 Calendar
c. 7-Eleven
b. 529 plan
d. Federal Home Loan Banks

35. _____ or financing is to provide capital (funds), which means money for a project, a person, a business or any other private or public institutions.

Those funds can be allocated for either short term or long term purposes. The health fund is a new way of _____ private healthcare centers.

a. Funding
c. Proxy fight
b. Product life cycle
d. Synthetic CDO

36. A _____ is a listing of bonds or fixed income instruments and a statistic reflecting the composite value of its components. It is used as a tool to represent the characteristics of its component fixed income instruments. They differ from stock market indices in their complexity.

a. 4-4-5 Calendar
c. 529 plan
b. 7-Eleven
d. Bond market index

Chapter 7. Mortgage Markets

37. _____s (_____s) are a form of securitization where payments from multiple middle sized and large business loans are pooled together and passed on to different classes of owners in various tranches.

Each class of owner may receive larger payments in exchange for being the first in line to lose money if the businesses fail to repay the loans. The actual loans used are generally multi-million dollar loans known as syndicated loans, usually originally lent by a bank with the intention of the loans being immediately paid off by the _____ owners.

   a. Tick size
   b. Fiscal sponsorship
   c. Financial rand
   d. Collateralized loan obligation

38. A _____ is a financial debt vehicle that was first created in June 1983 by investment banks Salomon Brothers and First Boston for Freddie Mac. (The First Boston team was led by Dexter Senft.) Legally, a _____ is a special purpose entity that is wholly separate from the institution(s) that create it.
   a. 4-4-5 Calendar
   b. Tranche
   c. Yield curve spread
   d. Collateralized mortgage obligation

39. In structured finance, a _____ is one of a number of related securities offered as part of the same transaction. The word _____ is French for slice, section, series, or portion. In the financial sense of the word, each bond is a different slice of the deal's risk.
   a. 4-4-5 Calendar
   b. Credit enhancement
   c. Yield curve spread
   d. Tranche

40. _____ is early repayment of a loan by a borrower.

In the case of a mortgage-backed security (MBS), _____ is perceived as a risk, because mortgage debts are often paid off early in order to incur lower total interest payments through cheaper refinancing. The new financing may be cheaper because the borrower's credit rating has improved or because interest rates are lower, but in either case, the payments that would have been made to the MBS investor would be above market rates.

   a. Bankruptcy remote
   b. Retention ratio
   c. Disposal tax effect
   d. Prepayment

41. _____ is a structured finance process that involves pooling and repackaging of cash-flow-producing financial assets into securities, which are then sold to investors. The term '_____' is derived from the fact that the form of financial instruments used to obtain funds from the investors are securities. As a portfolio risk backed by amortizing cash flows - and unlike general corporate debt - the credit quality of securitized debt is non-stationary due to changes in volatility that are time- and structure-dependent.
   a. The Glass-Steagall Act of 1933
   b. Reputational risk
   c. Special journals
   d. Securitization

Chapter 8. Foreign Exchange Markets

1. The _____ is where currency trading takes place. It is where banks and other official institutions facilitate the buying and selling of foreign currencies. FX transactions typically involve one party purchasing a quantity of one currency in exchange for paying a quantity of another.
   a. Floating exchange rate
   b. Spot market
   c. Foreign exchange option
   d. Foreign exchange market

2. A _____ is a fungible, negotiable instrument representing financial value. They are broadly categorized into debt securities (such as banknotes, bonds and debentures), and equity securities; e.g., common stocks. The company or other entity issuing the _____ is called the issuer.
   a. Book entry
   b. Security
   c. Securities lending
   d. Tracking stock

3. In finance, a _____ is a debt security, in which the authorized issuer owes the holders a debt and, depending on the terms of the _____, is obliged to pay interest (the coupon) and/or to repay the principal at a later date, termed maturity.

   Thus a _____ is a loan: the issuer is the borrower, the _____ holder is the lender, and the coupon is the interest. _____s provide the borrower with external funds to finance long-term investments, or, in the case of government _____s, to finance current expenditure.

   a. Convertible bond
   b. Bond
   c. Puttable bond
   d. Catastrophe bonds

4. The _____ is a financial market where participants buy and sell debt securities, usually in the form of bonds. As of 2006, the size of the international _____ is an estimated $45 trillion, of which the size of the outstanding U.S. _____ debt was $25.2 trillion.

   Nearly all of the $923 billion average daily trading volume in the U.S. _____ takes place between broker-dealers and large institutions in a decentralized, over-the-counter market.

   a. Fixed income
   b. Bond market
   c. 529 plan
   d. 4-4-5 Calendar

5. The _____ of monetary management established the rules for commercial and financial relations among the world's major industrial states in the mid 20th Century. The _____ was the first example of a fully negotiated monetary order intended to govern monetary relations among independent nation-states.

   Preparing to rebuild the international economic system as World War II was still raging, 730 delegates from all 44 Allied nations gathered at the Mount Washington Hotel in Bretton Woods, New Hampshire, United States, for the United Nations Monetary and Financial Conference.

   a. Fixed Asset Register
   b. The Hong Kong Securities Institute
   c. Cash budget
   d. Bretton Woods System

6. _____ is the loss of value of a country's currency with respect to one or more foreign reference currencies, typically in a floating exchange rate system. It is most often used for the unofficial increase of the exchange rate due to market forces, though sometimes it appears interchangeably with devaluation. Its opposite is called appreciation.

a. 529 plan
b. 7-Eleven
c. 4-4-5 Calendar
d. Currency depreciation

7. When companies conduct business across borders, they must deal in foreign currencies. Companies must exchange foreign currencies for home currencies when dealing with receivables, and vice versa for payables. This is done at the current exchange rate between the two countries. _____ is the risk that the exchange rate will change unfavorably before the currency is exchanged.

a. Lower of cost or market rule
b. 4-4-5 Calendar
c. 529 plan
d. Foreign exchange risk

8. The _____ was a December 1971 agreement that ended the fixed exchange rates established at the Bretton Woods Conference of 1944.

The Bretton Woods Conference of 1944 established an international fixed exchange rate regime in which currencies were pegged to the United States dollar, which was based on the gold standard.

By 1970, however, it was clear that the exchange rate regime was under threat, as the United States dollar was greatly overvalued because of heavy American spending on Lyndon B. Johnson's Great Society and the Vietnam War.

a. 7-Eleven
b. 4-4-5 Calendar
c. 529 plan
d. Smithsonian Agreement

9. _____ is a term used in accounting relating to the increase in value of an asset. In this sense it is the reverse of depreciation, which measures the fall in value of assets over their normal life-time.

_____ is a rise of a currency in a floating exchange rate.

a. Other Comprehensive Basis of Accounting
b. Appreciation
c. A Random Walk Down Wall Street
d. Operating cash flow

10. _____ is a term used in accounting, economics and finance to spread the cost of an asset over the span of several years.

In simple words we can say that _____ is the reduction in the value of an asset due to usage, passage of time, wear and tear, technological outdating or obsolescence, depletion or other such factors.

In accounting, _____ is a term used to describe any method of attributing the historical or purchase cost of an asset across its useful life, roughly corresponding to normal wear and tear.

a. Deferred financing costs
b. Depreciation
c. Bottom line
d. Matching principle

11. The _____ is an American financial and commodity derivative exchange based in Chicago. The _____ was founded in 1898 as the Chicago Butter and Egg Board. Originally, the exchange was a non-profit organization.

a. Gamelan Council
b. Financial Crimes Enforcement Network
c. Chicago Mercantile Exchange
d. Public Company Accounting Oversight Board

12. The _____ is the over-the-counter financial market in contracts for future delivery, so called forward contracts. Forward contracts are personalized between parties. The _____ is a general term used to describe the informal market by which these contracts are entered into.
   a. Forward market
   b. Spot rate
   c. Limits to arbitrage
   d. Delta hedging

13. In finance, a _____ is a standardized contract, to buy or sell a specified commodity of standardized quality at a certain date in the future, at a market determined price (the futures price.)

The price is determined by the instantaneous equilibrium between the forces of supply and demand among competing buy and sell orders on the exchange at the time of the purchase or sale of the contract.

In many cases, the items may be such non-traditional 'commodities' as foreign currencies, commercial or government paper [e.g., bonds], or 'baskets' of corporate equity ['stock indices'] or other financial instruments.

   a. Futures contract
   b. Financial future
   c. Repurchase agreement
   d. Heston model

14. In finance, the _____ is the global financial market for short-term borrowing and lending. It provides short-term liquidity funding for the global financial system. The _____ is where short-term obligations such as Treasury bills, commercial paper and bankers' acceptances are bought and sold.
   a. Debt-for-equity swap
   b. Cramdown
   c. Money Market
   d. Consumer debt

15. A _____, securities exchange or (in Europe) bourse is a corporation or mutual organization which provides 'trading' facilities for stock brokers and traders, to trade stocks and other securities. _____s also provide facilities for the issue and redemption of securities as well as other financial instruments and capital events including the payment of income and dividends. The securities traded on a _____ include: shares issued by companies, unit trusts and other pooled investment products and bonds.
   a. 529 plan
   b. 4-4-5 Calendar
   c. 7-Eleven
   d. Stock Exchange

16. A _____ is a bond issued by a corporation. The term is usually applied to longer-term debt instruments, generally with a maturity date falling at least a year after their issue date. (The term 'commercial paper' is sometimes used for instruments with a shorter maturity.)
   a. Government bond
   b. Corporate bond
   c. Serial bond
   d. Brady bonds

17. A _____, reserve bank, or monetary authority is the entity responsible for the monetary policy of a country or of a group of member states. It is a bank that can lend money to other banks in times of need. Its primary responsibility is to maintain the stability of the national currency and money supply, but more active duties include controlling subsidized-loan interest rates, and acting as a lender of last resort to the banking sector during times of financial crisis (private banks often being integral to the national financial system.)

Chapter 8. Foreign Exchange Markets

a. Central Bank
b. 4-4-5 Calendar
c. 529 plan
d. 7-Eleven

18. In finance, the _____ between two currencies specifies how much one currency is worth in terms of the other. For example an _____ of 102 Japanese yen to the United States dollar means that JPY 102 is worth the same as USD 1. The foreign exchange market is one of the largest markets in the world.
   a. AAB
   b. ABN Amro
   c. A Random Walk Down Wall Street
   d. Exchange rate

19. A _____ is a listing of bonds or fixed income instruments and a statistic reflecting the composite value of its components. It is used as a tool to represent the characteristics of its component fixed income instruments. They differ from stock market indices in their complexity.
   a. 7-Eleven
   b. 4-4-5 Calendar
   c. 529 plan
   d. Bond market index

20. _____ is the discipline of identifying, monitoring and limiting risks. In some cases the acceptable risk may be near zero. Risks can come from accidents, natural causes and disasters as well as deliberate attacks from an adversary.
   a. Penny stock
   b. Risk management
   c. 4-4-5 Calendar
   d. FIFO

21. A _____ is a foreign exchange agreement between two parties to exchange principal and fixed rate interest payments on a loan in one currency for principal and fixed rate interest payments on an equal (regarding net present value) loan in another currency. They are motivated by comparative advantage.
   a. Foreign exchange market
   b. Forex swap
   c. Currency pair
   d. Currency swap

22. A _____ is a financial contract whose value is derived from the value of something else (known as the underlying.) The underlying on which a _____ is based can be an asset, weather conditions bonds or other forms of credit.
   a. 529 plan
   b. 7-Eleven
   c. 4-4-5 Calendar
   d. Derivative

23. In finance, a _____ is a derivative in which two counterparties agree to exchange one stream of cash flows against another stream. These streams are called the legs of the _____.

The cash flows are calculated over a notional principal amount, which is usually not exchanged between counterparties.

   a. Local volatility
   b. Swap
   c. Volatility swap
   d. Volatility arbitrage

24. A _____ is an agreement between two parties to buy or sell an asset at a specified point of time in the future. The price of the underlying instrument, in whatever form, is paid before control of the instrument changes. This is one of the many forms of buy/sell orders where the time of trade is not the time where the securities themselves are exchanged.

a. Constant maturity credit default swap
b. Derivatives markets
c. Loan Credit Default Swap Index
d. Forward contract

25. _____ is a structured finance process that involves pooling and repackaging of cash-flow-producing financial assets into securities, which are then sold to investors. The term '_____' is derived from the fact that the form of financial instruments used to obtain funds from the investors are securities. As a portfolio risk backed by amortizing cash flows - and unlike general corporate debt - the credit quality of securitized debt is non-stationary due to changes in volatility that are time- and structure-dependent.
   a. Securitization
   b. The Glass-Steagall Act of 1933
   c. Reputational risk
   d. Special journals

26. A _____ is an exchange of promises between two or more parties to do an act which is enforceable in a court of law. It is where an unqualified offer meets a qualified acceptance and the parties reach Consensus ad Idem. The parties must have the necessary capacity to _____ and the _____ must not be either trifling, indeterminate, impossible or illegal.
   a. 4-4-5 Calendar
   b. 7-Eleven
   c. Contract
   d. 529 plan

27. _____ has become the norm for individual investors and traders over the past decade with many, if not all brokers now offering online services with unique trading platforms.

In the past, investors had to call up their brokers and place an order on the phone. The broker would then enter the order in their system which was linked to trading floors and exchanges.

   a. Alternative investment
   b. Asset allocation
   c. Investment decisions
   d. Investing online

28. The _____ is a United States government corporation created by the Glass-Steagall Act of 1933. It provides deposit insurance, which guarantees the safety of checking and savings deposits in member banks, currently up to $250,000 per depositor per bank. Insured deposits are backed by the full faith and credit of the United States.
   a. NYSE Group
   b. FASB
   c. Ford Foundation
   d. Federal Deposit Insurance Corporation

29. The _____ is published by The Economist as an informal way of measuring the purchasing power parity (PPP) between two currencies and provides a test of the extent to which market exchange rates result in goods costing the same in different countries. It 'seeks to make exchange-rate theory a bit more digestible'.
   a. 4-4-5 Calendar
   b. Divisia index
   c. 529 plan
   d. Big Mac index

30. _____ is a fee paid on borrowed assets. It is the price paid for the use of borrowed money , or, money earned by deposited funds . Assets that are sometimes lent with _____ include money, shares, consumer goods through hire purchase, major assets such as aircraft, and even entire factories in finance lease arrangements.
   a. A Random Walk Down Wall Street
   b. AAB
   c. Interest
   d. Insolvency

Chapter 8. Foreign Exchange Markets

31. An _____ is the price a borrower pays for the use of money they do not own, and the return a lender receives for deferring the use of funds, by lending it to the borrower. _____s are normally expressed as a percentage rate over the period of one year.

_____s targets are also a vital tool of monetary policy and are used to control variables like investment, inflation, and unemployment.

a. AAB
b. A Random Walk Down Wall Street
c. ABN Amro
d. Interest rate

32. _____ is an economic concept, expressed as a basic algebraic identity that relates interest rates and exchange rates. The identity is theoretical, and usually follows from assumptions imposed in economics models. There is evidence to support as well as to refute the concept.
a. Unit price
b. AAB
c. A Random Walk Down Wall Street
d. Interest rate parity

33. The _____ is an economic law stated as: 'In an efficient market all identical goods must have only one price.'

The intuition for this law is that all sellers will flock to the highest prevailing price, and all buyers to the lowest current market price. In an efficient market the convergence on one price is instant.

Commodities can be traded on financial markets, where there will be a single offer price, and bid price.

a. Letter of credit
b. Personal property
c. Liability
d. Law of one price

34. _____, in bookkeeping, refers to assets, liabilities, income, and expenses recorded on individual pages of the so called book of final entry or ledger. Changes in _____ value are made by chronologically posting debit (DR) and credit (CR) entries to its page. Examples of _____s are cash, _____s receivable, mortgages, loans, land and buildings, common stock, sales, services provided, wages, and payroll overhead.
a. Accretion
b. Account
c. Option
d. Alpha

Chapter 9. Stock Markets

1. A _____ is a fungible, negotiable instrument representing financial value. They are broadly categorized into debt securities (such as banknotes, bonds and debentures), and equity securities; e.g., common stocks. The company or other entity issuing the _____ is called the issuer.
   - a. Book entry
   - b. Tracking stock
   - c. Securities lending
   - d. Security

2. A _____ is a private or public market for the trading of company stock and derivatives of company stock at an agreed price; these are securities listed on a stock exchange as well as those only traded privately.

   The size of the world _____ is estimated at about $36.6 trillion US at the beginning of October 2008 . The world derivatives market has been estimated at about $480 trillion face or nominal value, 12 times the size of the entire world economy.

   - a. Anton Gelonkin
   - b. Adolph Coors
   - c. Andrew Tobias
   - d. Stock market

3. In finance, a _____ is a debt security, in which the authorized issuer owes the holders a debt and, depending on the terms of the _____, is obliged to pay interest (the coupon) and/or to repay the principal at a later date, termed maturity.

   Thus a _____ is a loan: the issuer is the borrower, the _____ holder is the lender, and the coupon is the interest. _____s provide the borrower with external funds to finance long-term investments, or, in the case of government _____s, to finance current expenditure.

   - a. Catastrophe bonds
   - b. Bond
   - c. Convertible bond
   - d. Puttable bond

4. The _____ is a financial market where participants buy and sell debt securities, usually in the form of bonds. As of 2006, the size of the international _____ is an estimated $45 trillion, of which the size of the outstanding U.S. _____ debt was $25.2 trillion.

   Nearly all of the $923 billion average daily trading volume in the U.S. _____ takes place between broker-dealers and large institutions in a decentralized, over-the-counter market.

   - a. Fixed income
   - b. 529 plan
   - c. 4-4-5 Calendar
   - d. Bond market

5. _____ is a form of corporation equity ownership represented in the securities. It is dangerous in comparison to preferred shares and some other investment options, in that in the event of bankruptcy, _____ investors receive their funds after preferred stockholders, bondholders, creditors, etc. On the other hand, common shares on average perform better than preferred shares or bonds over time.
   - a. Stock split
   - b. Stop-limit order
   - c. Stock market bubble
   - d. Common stock

6. A _____ is a payment made by a corporation to its shareholder members. When a corporation earns a profit or surplus, that money can be put to two uses: it can either be re-invested in the business (called retained earnings), or it can be paid to the shareholders as a _____. Many corporations retain a portion of their earnings and pay the remainder as a _____.

   a. Special dividend
   b. Dividend
   c. Dividend yield
   d. Dividend puzzle

7. _____ are those dividends paid out in form of additional stock shares of the issuing corporation or other corporation They are usually issued in proportion to shares owned (for example for every 100 shares of stock owned, 5% stock dividend will yield 5 extra shares). If this payment involves the issue of new shares, this is very similar to a stock split in that it increases the total number of shares while lowering the price of each share and does not change the market capitalization or the total value of the shares held

   a. Stock or scrip dividends
   b. Time-based currency
   c. The Hong Kong Securities Institute
   d. Database auditing

8. _____ is a concept whereby a person's financial liability is limited to a fixed sum, most commonly the value of a person's investment in a company or partnership with _____. A shareholder in a limited company is not personally liable for any of the debts of the company, other than for the value of his investment in that company. The same is true for the members of a _____ partnership and the limited partners in a limited partnership.

   a. Beneficial owner
   b. Personal property
   c. Sarbanes-Oxley Act
   d. Limited liability

9. In the most general sense, a _____ is anything that is a hindrance, or puts individuals at a disadvantage.

   Before we discuss the financial terms, we should note that a _____ can also have a much more important slang meaning.

   This is best described in an example.

   a. Limited liability
   b. Covenant
   c. McFadden Act
   d. Liability

10. _____ is a multiple-winner voting system intended to promote proportional representation while also being simple to understand.

    _____ is used frequently in corporate governance, where it is mandated by many U.S. states, and it was used to elect the Illinois House of Representatives from 1870 until its repeal in 1980. It was used in England in the late 19th century to elect school boards.

    a. 7-Eleven
    b. 529 plan
    c. 4-4-5 Calendar
    d. Cumulative voting

11. _____ is capital stock which provides a specific dividend that is paid before any dividends are paid to common stock holders, and which takes precedence over common stock in the event of a liquidation. This form of financing is used by private equity investors and venture capital firms. Holders of _____ get both their money back (with interest) and the money that is distributable with respect to the percentage of common shares into which their preferred stock can convert.

Chapter 9. Stock Markets

a. Preferred stock
c. Cash is king
b. Shareholder value
d. Participating preferred stock

12. _____ is typically a higher ranking stock than voting shares, and its terms are negotiated between the corporation and the investor.

_____ usually carry no voting rights, but may carry superior priority over common stock in the payment of dividends and upon liquidation. _____ may carry a dividend that is paid out prior to any dividends to common stock holders.

a. Follow-on offering
c. Second lien loan
b. Preferred stock
d. Trade-off theory

13. The _____ is that part of the capital markets that deals with the issuance of new securities. Companies, governments or public sector institutions can obtain funding through the sale of a new stock or bond issue. This is typically done through a syndicate of securities dealers.

a. Sector rotation
c. Peer group analysis
b. Volatility clustering
d. Primary market

14. _____, is when a company issues common stock or shares to the public for the first time. They are often issued by smaller, younger companies seeking capital to expand, but can also be done by large privately-owned companies looking to become publicly traded.

In an _____ the issuer may obtain the assistance of an underwriting firm, which helps it determine what type of security to issue (common or preferred), best offering price and time to bring it to market.

a. Asian Financial Crisis
c. Interest
b. Initial public offering
d. Insolvency

15. In business and finance, a _____ (also referred to as equity _____) of stock means a _____ of ownership in a corporation (company.) In the plural, stocks is often used as a synonym for _____s especially in the United States, but it is less commonly used that way outside of North America.

In the United Kingdom, South Africa, and Australia, stock can also refer to completely different financial instruments such as government bonds or, less commonly, to all kinds of marketable securities.

a. Bucket shop
c. Procter ' Gamble
b. Margin
d. Share

16. A _____ is a right to acquire certain property in preference to any other person. It usually refers to property newly coming into existence. A right to acquire existing property in preference to any other person is usually referred to as a right of first refusal.

In practice, the most common form of _____ is the right of existing shareholders to acquire newly issued shares issued by a company in a rights issue, a usually but not always public offering.

a. Fraud deterrence
b. Court of Audit of Belgium
c. Down payment
d. Pre-emption right

17. The U.S. _____ is an independent agency of the United States government which holds primary responsibility for enforcing the federal securities laws and regulating the securities industry, the nation's stock and options exchanges, and other electronic securities markets. The SEC was created by section 4 of the SEC of 1934 (now codified as 15 U.S.C. § 78d and commonly referred to as the 1934 Act.)

a. 7-Eleven
b. 4-4-5 Calendar
c. 529 plan
d. Securities and Exchange Commission

18. A _____ is a financial contract whose value is derived from the value of something else (known as the underlying.) The underlying on which a _____ is based can be an asset, weather conditions bonds or other forms of credit.

a. 529 plan
b. 4-4-5 Calendar
c. 7-Eleven
d. Derivative

19. The term _____, also known as a waiting period is a period extended from the time a company files a registration statement with the SEC until SEC staff declared the registration statement effective. During that period, the federal securities laws limited what information a company and related parties can release to the public.'

Under the rules of the Securities Act of 1933, as modified June 29, 2005, electronic communications, including electronic road shows and information located on or hyperlinked to an issuer's website are also governed. The rules changes of June 29, 2005 also included various changes which 'liberalize permitted offering activity and communications to allow more information' for certain qualifying organizations.

a. Duty of loyalty
b. Lien
c. Leasing
d. Quiet period

20. In the United States, the Financial Industry Regulatory Authority (FINRA) is a self-regulatory organization (SRO) under the Securities Exchange Act of 1934, successor to the _____.

FINRA is responsible for regulatory oversight of all securities firms that do business with the public; professional training, testing and licensing of registered persons; arbitration and mediation; market regulation by contract for The NASDAQ Stock Market, Inc., the American Stock Exchange LLC, and the International Securities Exchange, LLC; and industry utilities, such as Trade Reporting Facilities and other over-the-counter operations.

a. 529 plan
b. 7-Eleven
c. 4-4-5 Calendar
d. NASD

21. In the United States, the Financial Industry Regulatory Authority (FINRA) is a self-regulatory organization (SRO) under the Securities Exchange Act of 1934, successor to the _____, Inc.

FINRA is responsible for regulatory oversight of all securities firms that do business with the public; professional training, testing and licensing of registered persons; arbitration and mediation; market regulation by contract for The NASDAQ Stock Market, Inc., the American Stock Exchange LLC, and the International Securities Exchange, LLC; and industry utilities, such as Trade Reporting Facilities and other over-the-counter operations.

Chapter 9. Stock Markets

a. 7-Eleven
b. 4-4-5 Calendar
c. 529 plan
d. National Association of Securities Dealers

22. _____ is an arrangement with the U.S. Securities and Exchange Commission that allows a single registration document to be filed that permits the issuance of multiple securities.

_____ is a registration of a new issue which can be prepared up to two years in advance, so that the issue can be offered quickly as soon as funds are needed or market conditions are favorable.

For example, current market conditions in the housing market are not favorable for a specific firm to issue a public offering.

a. Bought deal
b. 4-4-5 Calendar
c. Shelf registration
d. Black Sea Trade and Development Bank

23. The _____ is the financial market where previously issued securities and financial instruments such as stock, bonds, options, and futures are bought and sold. The term '_____' is also used refer to the market for any used goods or assets, or an alternative use for an existing product or asset where the customer base is the second market

With primary issuances of securities or financial instruments, or the primary market, investors purchase these securities directly from issuers such as corporations issuing shares in an IPO or private placement, or directly from the federal government in the case of treasuries.

a. Delta neutral
b. Performance attribution
c. Financial market
d. Secondary market

24. The _____ is an American stock exchange. It is the largest electronic screen-based equity securities trading market in the United States. With approximately 3,200 companies, it has more trading volume per day than any other stock exchange in the world.

a. 4-4-5 Calendar
b. 7-Eleven
c. 529 plan
d. NASDAQ

25. The _____ is a stock exchange based in New York City, New York. It is the largest stock exchange in the world by dollar value of its listed companies securities. As of October 2008, the combined capitalization of all domestic _____ listed companies was $10.1 trillion.

a. 4-4-5 Calendar
b. 529 plan
c. 7-Eleven
d. New York Stock Exchange

26. A _____, securities exchange or (in Europe) bourse is a corporation or mutual organization which provides 'trading' facilities for stock brokers and traders, to trade stocks and other securities. _____s also provide facilities for the issue and redemption of securities as well as other financial instruments and capital events including the payment of income and dividends. The securities traded on a _____ include: shares issued by companies, unit trusts and other pooled investment products and bonds.

a. Stock Exchange
b. 4-4-5 Calendar
c. 529 plan
d. 7-Eleven

Chapter 9. Stock Markets

27. A _____ is a bond issued by a corporation. The term is usually applied to longer-term debt instruments, generally with a maturity date falling at least a year after their issue date. (The term 'commercial paper' is sometimes used for instruments with a shorter maturity.)

  a. Brady bonds
  b. Government bond
  c. Serial bond
  d. Corporate bond

28. A _____ is an order to buy a security at no more (or sell at no less) than a specific price. This gives the customer some control over the price at which the trade is executed, but may prevent the order from being executed ('filled'.)

A buy _____ can only be executed by the broker at the limit price or lower.

  a. Common stock
  b. Block premium
  c. Commercial mortgage-backed securities
  d. Limit order

29. A _____ is a buy or sell order to be executed by the broker immediately at current market prices. As long as there are willing sellers and buyers, _____s are filled.

A _____ is the simplest of the order types.

  a. Trading curb
  b. Stockholder
  c. Block premium
  d. Market order

30. A _____ is a point at which a stock market will stop trading for a period of time in response to substantial drops in value.

On the New York Stock Exchange, one type of _____ is referred to as a 'circuit breaker.' These limits were put in place after Black Monday in order to reduce market volatility and massive panic sell-offs, giving traders time to reconsider their transactions.

At the start of each quarter, the NYSE sets three circuit breaker levels at levels of 10%, 20%, and 30% of the average closing price of the Dow Jones Industrial Average for the month preceding the start of the quarter, rounded to the nearest 50-point interval.

  a. Common stock
  b. Stock repurchase
  c. Stock market index
  d. Trading curb

31. _____ is casually defined as the use of computers in stock markets to engage in arbitrage and portfolio insurance strategies. However, the New York Stock Exchange (NYSE) defines the term as 'a wide range of portfolio trading strategies involving the purchase or sale of 15 or more stocks having a total market value of $1 million or more' without any direct reference to the use of computers. The word 'program' can be interpreted in its earlier, more general meaning of a defined and pre-arranged sequence of steps, rather than specifically a computer program.

  a. Wash sale
  b. Share price
  c. Program trading
  d. Stop order

Chapter 9. Stock Markets

32. A _____ is a listing of bonds or fixed income instruments and a statistic reflecting the composite value of its components. It is used as a tool to represent the characteristics of its component fixed income instruments. They differ from stock market indices in their complexity.
    a. Bond market index
    b. 7-Eleven
    c. 4-4-5 Calendar
    d. 529 plan

33. The _____ is an electronic quotation system in the United States that displays real-time quotes, last-sale prices, and volume information for many over-the-counter (OTC) equity securities that are not listed on the NASDAQ stock exchange or a national securities exchange. Broker-dealers who subscribe to the system can use the _____ to look up prices or enter quotes for OTC securities.
    a. OTC bulletin board
    b. Insolvency
    c. Internal control
    d. AT'T Inc.

34. An _____ is the term used in financial circles for a type of computer system that facilitates trading of financial products outside of stock exchanges. The primary products that are traded on an _____ are stocks and currencies. They came into existence in 1998 when the SEC authorized their creation.
    a. Open outcry
    b. Insider trading
    c. Intellidex
    d. Electronic communication network

35. A _____ is a method of measuring a section of the stock market. Many indices are cited by news or financial services firms and are used to benchmark the performance of portfolios such as mutual funds.
    a. Program trading
    b. Trading curb
    c. Stop order
    d. Stock market index

36. The _____ is one of several stock market indices, created by nineteenth-century Wall Street Journal editor and Dow Jones ' Company co-founder Charles Dow. Dow compiled the index to gauge the performance of the industrial sector of the American stock market. It is the second-oldest U.S. market index, after the Dow Jones Transportation Average, which Dow also created.
    a. 529 plan
    b. 4-4-5 Calendar
    c. 7-Eleven
    d. Dow Jones Industrial Average

37. A _____ index is a stock market index where each constituent makes up a fraction of the index that is proportional to its price. For a stock market index this implies that stocks are included in proportions based on their quoted prices. A stock trading at $100 will thus be making up 10 times more of the total index compared to a stock trading at $10.
    a. Golden parachute
    b. Price-weighted
    c. Trade finance
    d. Product life cycle

38. An _____ (or business indicator) is a statistic about the economy. _____s allow analysis of economic performance and predictions of future performance.

    _____s include various indices, earnings reports, and economic summaries, such as unemployment, housing starts, Consumer Price Index (a measure for inflation), industrial production, bankruptcies, Gross Domestic Product, broadband internet penetration, retail sales, stock market prices, and money supply changes.

a. Economic indicator
b. AAB
c. A Random Walk Down Wall Street
d. ABN Amro

39. _____ is the trading of a corporation's stock or other securities (e.g. bonds or stock options) by individuals with potential access to non-public information about the company. In most countries, trading by corporate insiders such as officers, key employees, directors, and large shareholders may be legal, if this trading is done in a way that does not take advantage of non-public information. However, the term is frequently used to refer to a practice in which an insider or a related party trades based on material non-public information obtained during the performance of the insider's duties at the corporation, or otherwise in breach of a fiduciary duty or other relationship of trust and confidence or where the non-public information was misappropriated from the company.
 a. Open outcry
 b. Intellidex
 c. Equity investment
 d. Insider trading

40. _____ is a regulation of the U.S. Securities and Exchange Commission It allows an issuer to sell securities without registering them with the SEC. Rule 501 contains definitions that apply to the rest of _____. Rule 502 contains the general conditions that must be met to take advantage of the exemptions under _____. Generally speaking, these conditions are that all sales within a certain time period that are part of the same Reg D offering must be 'integrated', information and disclosures must be provided, there must be no 'general solicitation', and that the securities being sold contain restrictions on their resale.
 a. 7-Eleven
 b. 4-4-5 Calendar
 c. Regulation D
 d. 529 plan

41. The U.S. Securities and Exchange Commission's (SEC's) Regulation Fair Disclosure, also commonly referred to as _____ was an SEC ruling implemented in October 2000 (.) It mandated that all publicly traded companies must disclose material information to all investors at the same time.

The regulation sought to stamp out selective disclosure, in which some investors (often large institutional investors) received market moving information before others (often smaller, individual investors.)

 a. Revenue recognition
 b. Regulation Fair Disclosure
 c. Regulation FD
 d. Commodity Pool Operator

42. Congress enacted the _____, in the aftermath of the stock market crash of 1929 and during the ensuing Great Depression. It requires that any offer or sale of securities using the means and instrumentalities of interstate commerce be registered pursuant to the 1933 Act, unless an exemption from registration exists under the law.
 a. Securities Act of 1933
 b. 4-4-5 Calendar
 c. 7-Eleven
 d. 529 plan

43. The _____ of 1934 is a law governing the secondary trading of securities (stocks, bonds, and debentures) in the United States of America. The Act, 48 Stat. 881 (enacted June 6, 1934), codified at 15 U.S.C. § 78a et seq., was a sweeping piece of legislation. The Act and related statutes form the basis of regulation of the financial markets and their participants in the United States.
 a. 7-Eleven
 b. 4-4-5 Calendar
 c. 529 plan
 d. Securities Exchange Act

Chapter 9. Stock Markets

44. _____ is the set of processes, customs, policies, laws and institutions affecting the way a corporation is directed, administered or controlled. _____ also includes the relationships among the many stakeholders involved and the goals for which the corporation is governed. The principal stakeholders are the shareholders, management and the board of directors.
   a. Corporate governance
   b. Foreign Corrupt Practices Act
   c. Due diligence
   d. Patent

45. _____ is the provision of resources (such as granting a loan) by one party to another party where that second party does not reimburse the first party immediately, thereby generating a debt, and instead arranges either to repay or return those resources (or material(s) of equal value) at a later date. The first party is called a creditor, also known as a lender, while the second party is called a debtor, also known as a borrower.

Movements of financial capital are normally dependent on either _____ or equity transfers.

   a. Comparable
   b. Warrant
   c. Credit
   d. Clearing house

46. The _____ of 2002 (Pub.L. 107-204, 116 Stat. 745, enacted July 30, 2002), also known as the Public Company Accounting Reform and Investor Protection Act of 2002 and commonly called Sarbanes-Oxley, Sarbox or SOX, is a United States federal law enacted on July 30, 2002 in response to a number of major corporate and accounting scandals including those affecting Enron, Tyco International, Adelphia, Peregrine Systems and WorldCom.
   a. Foreign Corrupt Practices Act
   b. Duty of loyalty
   c. Sarbanes-Oxley Act
   d. Blue sky law

47. _____ is a measurement of corporate or economic size equal to the share price times the number of shares outstanding of a public company. As owning stock represents owning the company, including all its equity, capitalization could represent the public opinion of a company's net worth and is a determining factor in stock valuation. Likewise, the capitalization of stock markets or economic regions may be compared to other economic indicators.
   a. Proxy fight
   b. Synthetic CDO
   c. Just-in-time
   d. Market capitalization

48. An _____ represents the ownership in the shares of a foreign company trading on US financial markets. The stock of many non-US companies trades on US exchanges through the use of _____s. _____s enable US investors to buy shares in foreign companies without undertaking cross-border transactions.
   a. AAB
   b. A Random Walk Down Wall Street
   c. American depository receipt
   d. ABN Amro

49. A _____ is a certificate issued by a depository bank, which purchases shares of foreign companies and deposits it on the account. _____s represent ownership of an underlying number of shares.

They facilitate trade of shares, and are commonly used to invest in companies from developing or emerging markets.

   a. Special journals
   b. The Security Industry Association
   c. Short positions
   d. Global depository receipt

Chapter 9. Stock Markets

50. The term _____ has three unrelated technical definitions, and is also used in a variety of non-technical ways.

- In financial economics, it refers to any asset used to make money, as opposed to assets used for personal enjoyment or consumption. This is an important distinction because two people can disagree sharply about the value of personal assets, one person might think a sports car is more valuable than a pickup truck, another person might have the opposite taste. But if an asset is held for the purpose of making money, taste has nothing to do with it, only differences of opinion about how much money the asset will produce. With the further assumption that people agree on the probability distribution of future cash flows, it is possible to have an objective _____ pricing model. Even without the assumption of agreement, it is possible to set rational limits on _____ value.
- In governmental accounting, it is defined as any asset used in operations with an initial useful life extending beyond one reporting period. Generally, government managers have a 'stewardship' duty to maintain _____s under their control. See International Public Sector Accounting Standards for details.
- In US tax accounting, it is defined as any property other than a list of exceptions. The main exceptions are anything held for sale, and any real estate or depreciable property used in business. Almost everything you own and use for personal purposes, pleasure or investment is a _____. If something is a _____ for tax purposes, gains or losses on sale or disposition are capital gains or capital losses. For individuals, however, capital losses on property held for personal use are generally not deductible. See the IRS publication Tax Facts about Capital Gains and Losses for details.

A well-known financial accounting textbook advises that the term be avoided except in tax accounting because it is used in so many different senses, not all of them well-defined. For example it is often used as a synonym for fixed assets or for investments in securities.

A common non-technical usage occurs when people ask that employees or the environment or something else be treated as a _____.

a. Political risk
b. Capital asset
c. Settlement date
d. Solvency

51. In finance, the _____ is used to determine a theoretically appropriate required rate of return of an asset, if that asset is to be added to an already well-diversified portfolio, given that asset's non-diversifiable risk. The model takes into account the asset's sensitivity to non-diversifiable risk (also known as systemic risk or market risk), often represented by the quantity beta (β) in the financial industry, as well as the expected return of the market and the expected return of a theoretical risk-free asset.

The model was introduced by Jack Treynor (1961, 1962), William Sharpe (1964), John Lintner (1965a,b) and Jan Mossin (1966) independently, building on the earlier work of Harry Markowitz on diversification and modern portfolio theory.

a. Capital asset pricing model
b. Hull-White model
c. Cox-Ingersoll-Ross model
d. Random walk hypothesis

Chapter 9. Stock Markets

52. An _____ is a statistical method to assess the impact of an event on the value of a firm. For example, the announcement of a merger between two firms can be analyzed to see whether investors believe the merger will create or destroy value. Event studies have been used in a large variety of studies, including [mergers and acquisitions], earnings announcements, debt or equity issues, corporate reorganisations, investment decisions and corporate social responsibility (MacKinlay 1997; McWilliams ' Siegel, 1997.)

   a. AAB
   b. Event study
   c. ABN Amro
   d. A Random Walk Down Wall Street

53. In business and accounting, _____s are everything of value that is owned by a person or company. The balance sheet of a firm records the monetary value of the _____s owned by the firm. The two major _____ classes are tangible _____s and intangible _____s.

   a. Accounts payable
   b. EBITDA
   c. Asset
   d. Income

54. In finance, _____ is the process of estimating the potential market value of a financial asset or liability. they can be done on assets (for example, investments in marketable securities such as stocks, options, business enterprises, or intangible assets such as patents and trademarks) or on liabilities (e.g., Bonds issued by a company.) _____s are required in many contexts including investment analysis, capital budgeting, merger and acquisition transactions, financial reporting, taxable events to determine the proper tax liability, and in litigation.

   a. Margin
   b. Share
   c. Procter ' Gamble
   d. Valuation

Chapter 10. Derivative Securities Markets

1. A _____ is a financial contract whose value is derived from the value of something else (known as the underlying.) The underlying on which a _____ is based can be an asset, weather conditions bonds or other forms of credit.
   a. 4-4-5 Calendar
   b. 529 plan
   c. 7-Eleven
   d. Derivative

2. A _____ is a fungible, negotiable instrument representing financial value. They are broadly categorized into debt securities (such as banknotes, bonds and debentures), and equity securities; e.g., common stocks. The company or other entity issuing the _____ is called the issuer.
   a. Book entry
   b. Tracking stock
   c. Securities lending
   d. Security

3. In finance, a _____ is a derivative in which two counterparties agree to exchange one stream of cash flows against another stream. These streams are called the legs of the _____.

   The cash flows are calculated over a notional principal amount, which is usually not exchanged between counterparties.

   a. Volatility swap
   b. Local volatility
   c. Swap
   d. Volatility arbitrage

4. In finance, a _____ is a debt security, in which the authorized issuer owes the holders a debt and, depending on the terms of the _____, is obliged to pay interest (the coupon) and/or to repay the principal at a later date, termed maturity.

   Thus a _____ is a loan: the issuer is the borrower, the _____ holder is the lender, and the coupon is the interest. _____ s provide the borrower with external funds to finance long-term investments, or, in the case of government _____ s, to finance current expenditure.

   a. Catastrophe bonds
   b. Convertible bond
   c. Puttable bond
   d. Bond

5. The _____ is a financial market where participants buy and sell debt securities, usually in the form of bonds. As of 2006, the size of the international _____ is an estimated $45 trillion, of which the size of the outstanding U.S. _____ debt was $25.2 trillion.

   Nearly all of the $923 billion average daily trading volume in the U.S. _____ takes place between broker-dealers and large institutions in a decentralized, over-the-counter market.

   a. Fixed income
   b. 529 plan
   c. 4-4-5 Calendar
   d. Bond market

6. _____ is a major futures and options exchange for European benchmark derivatives featuring open and low-cost electronic access globally. Its electronic trading and clearing platform offers a broad range of products and amongst other, operates the most liquid fixed income markets. _____ was established in 1998 with the merger of Deutsche Terminbörse and SOFFEX (Swiss Options and Financial Futures.)

Chapter 10. Derivative Securities Markets

a. Eurex
c. AAB

b. A Random Walk Down Wall Street
d. ABN Amro

7. _____ is the name of a method of communication between professionals on a stock exchange or futures exchange which involves shouting and the use of hand signals to transfer information primarily about buy and sell orders. The part of the trading floor where this takes place is called a pit.

Examples of markets which use this system in the United States are the New York Mercantile Exchange, the Chicago Mercantile Exchange, the Chicago Board of Trade, and the Chicago Board Options Exchange.

a. Intellidex
c. Insider trading

b. Equity investment
d. Open outcry

8. A _____ is a bond issued by a corporation. The term is usually applied to longer-term debt instruments, generally with a maturity date falling at least a year after their issue date. (The term 'commercial paper' is sometimes used for instruments with a shorter maturity.)

a. Serial bond
c. Government bond

b. Brady bonds
d. Corporate bond

9. A _____ is an agreement between two parties to buy or sell an asset at a specified point of time in the future. The price of the underlying instrument, in whatever form, is paid before control of the instrument changes. This is one of the many forms of buy/sell orders where the time of trade is not the time where the securities themselves are exchanged.

a. Derivatives markets
c. Loan Credit Default Swap Index

b. Forward contract
d. Constant maturity credit default swap

10. _____ is the discipline of identifying, monitoring and limiting risks. In some cases the acceptable risk may be near zero. Risks can come from accidents, natural causes and disasters as well as deliberate attacks from an adversary.

a. 4-4-5 Calendar
c. Penny stock

b. Risk management
d. FIFO

11. A _____ is an exchange of promises between two or more parties to do an act which is enforceable in a court of law. It is where an unqualified offer meets a qualified acceptance and the parties reach Consensus ad Idem. The parties must have the necessary capacity to _____ and the _____ must not be either trifling, indeterminate, impossible or illegal.

a. 4-4-5 Calendar
c. 7-Eleven

b. 529 plan
d. Contract

12. The _____ or cash market is a commodities or securities market in which goods are sold for cash and delivered immediately. Contracts bought and sold on these markets are immediately effective. _____s can operate wherever the infrastructure exists to conduct the transaction.

a. Foreign exchange controls
c. Spot market

b. Currency swap
d. Non-deliverable forward

13. In finance, a _____ is a standardized contract, to buy or sell a specified commodity of standardized quality at a certain date in the future, at a market determined price (the futures price.)

The price is determined by the instantaneous equilibrium between the forces of supply and demand among competing buy and sell orders on the exchange at the time of the purchase or sale of the contract.

In many cases, the items may be such non-traditional 'commodities' as foreign currencies, commercial or government paper [e.g., bonds], or 'baskets' of corporate equity ['stock indices'] or other financial instruments.

   a. Futures contract
   c. Heston model
   b. Financial future
   d. Repurchase agreement

14. A _____ is a central financial exchange where people can trade standardized futures contracts; that is, a contract to buy specific quantities of a commodity or financial instrument at a specified price with delivery set at a specified time in the future.

Though the origins of futures trading can supposedly be traced to Ancient Greek or Phoenician times, the first modern organized _____ began in 1710 at the Dojima Rice Exchange in Osaka, Japan.

The United States followed in the early 1800s.

   a. 529 plan
   c. 7-Eleven
   b. 4-4-5 Calendar
   d. Futures Exchange

15. _____ or fair value accounting refers to the accounting standards of assigning a value to a position held in a financial instrument based on the current fair market price for the instrument or similar instruments. Fair value accounting has been a part of US Generally Accepted Accounting Principles (GAAP) since the early 1990s. The use of fair value measurements has increased steadily over the past decade, primarily in response to investor demand for relevant and timely financial statements that will aid in making better informed decisions.

   a. 529 plan
   c. Mark-to-market
   b. 4-4-5 Calendar
   d. 7-Eleven

16. The _____ requirement is the amount required to be collateralized in order to open a position. Thereafter, the amount required to be kept in collateral until the position is closed is the maintenance requirement. The maintenance requirement is the minimum amount to be collateralized in order to keep an open position.

   a. Initial margin
   c. Efficient-market hypothesis
   b. Arbitrage
   d. Issuer

17. The variation margin or _____ is not collateral, but a daily offsetting of profits and losses. Futures are marked-to-market every day, so the current price is compared to the previous day's price. The profit or loss on the day of a position is then paid to or debited from the holder by the futures exchange.

   a. Delivery month
   c. SPI 200 futures contract
   b. Total return swap
   d. Maintenance margin

Chapter 10. Derivative Securities Markets

18. In finance, a _____ is collateral that the holder of a position in securities, options, or futures contracts has to deposit to cover the credit risk of his counterparty (most often his broker.) This risk can arise if the holder has done any of the following:

- borrowed cash from the counterparty to buy securities or options,
- sold securities or options short, or
- entered into a futures contract.

The collateral can be in the form of cash or securities, and it is deposited in a _____ account. On U.S. futures exchanges, '_____' was formally called performance bond.

_____ buying is buying securities with cash borrowed from a broker, using other securities as collateral.

a. Credit
c. Procter ' Gamble
b. Share
d. Margin

19. The _____ is an American financial and commodity derivative exchange based in Chicago. The _____ was founded in 1898 as the Chicago Butter and Egg Board. Originally, the exchange was a non-profit organization.
a. Public Company Accounting Oversight Board
b. Gamelan Council
c. Financial Crimes Enforcement Network
d. Chicago Mercantile Exchange

20. In the original and simplified sense, _____ were things of value, of uniform quality, that were produced in large quantities by many different producers; the items from each different producer are considered equivalent. It is the contract and this underlying standard that define the commodity, not any quality inherent in the product.

_____ exchanges include:

- Chicago Board of Trade
- Kansas City Board of Trade
- Euronext.liffe
- Kuala Lumpur Futures Exchange
- Bhatinda Om ' Oil Exchange
- London Metal Exchange
- New York Mercantile Exchange
- Multi Commodity Exchange
- Dalian Commodity Exchange

Markets for trading _____ can be very efficient, particularly if the division into pools matches demand segments. These markets will quickly respond to changes in supply and demand to find an equilibrium price and quantity.

a. 4-4-5 Calendar
c. 7-Eleven
b. 529 plan
d. Commodities

Chapter 10. Derivative Securities Markets

21. In finance, the _____ is the global financial market for short-term borrowing and lending. It provides short-term liquidity funding for the global financial system. The _____ is where short-term obligations such as Treasury bills, commercial paper and bankers' acceptances are bought and sold.
   a. Debt-for-equity swap
   b. Money Market
   c. Consumer debt
   d. Cramdown

22. A _____ is a trader who buys and sells financial instruments (eg stocks, options, futures, derivatives, currencies) within the same trading day such that all positions will usually be closed before the market close of the trading day. This trading style is called day trading. Depending on one's trading strategy, it may range from several to hundreds of orders a day.
   a. Financial analyst
   b. Stockbroker
   c. Portfolio manager
   d. Day trader

23. A _____ is a member of an exchange who is an employee of a member firm and executes orders, as agent, on the floor of the exchange for clients. The _____ receives an order via teletype machine from his firm's trading department and then proceeds to the appropriate trading post on the exchange floor. There he joins other brokers and the specialist in the security being bought or sold and executes the trade at the best competitive price available.
   a. Case-Shiller Home Price Indices
   b. Multivariate normal distribution
   c. Business valuation standards
   d. Floor broker

24. _____ are government bonds issued by the United States Department of the Treasury through the Bureau of the Public Debt. They are the debt financing instruments of the U.S. Federal government, and they are often referred to simply as Treasuries or Treasurys. There are four types of marketable _____: Treasury bills, Treasury notes, Treasury bonds, and Treasury Inflation Protected Securities (TIPS.)
   a. Treasury Inflation-Protected Securities
   b. Treasury securities
   c. 4-4-5 Calendar
   d. Treasury Inflation Protected Securities

25. A _____ is a financial services company that provides clearing and settlement services for financial transactions, usually on a futures exchange, and often acts as central counterparty (the payor actually pays the _____, which then pays the payee). A _____ may also offer novation, the substitution of a new contract or debt for an old, or other credit enhancement services to its members.

The term is also used for banks like Suffolk Bank that acted as a restraint on the over-issuance of private bank notes.

   a. Valuation
   b. Bucket shop
   c. Warrant
   d. Clearing house

26. In finance, a _____ in a security, such as a stock or a bond means the holder of the position owns the security and will profit if the price of the security goes up.

Similarly, a _____ in a futures contract or similar derivative, means the holder of the position will profit if the price of the underlying security goes up. Going long is the more conventional practice of investing and is contrasted with going short

Chapter 10. Derivative Securities Markets

- Short (finance)

a. Forward market
b. Central Securities Depository
c. Long position
d. Delta hedging

27. Days to Cover (DTC) is a numerical term that describes the relationship between the amount of shares in a given equity that have been short sold and the number of days of typical trading that it would require to 'cover' all _____ outstanding. For example, if there are ten million shares of XYZ Inc. that are currently short sold and the average daily volume of XYZ shares traded each day is one million, it would require ten days of trading for all _____ to be covered (10 million / 1 million.)
a. Cash budget
b. Stock or scrip dividends
c. Guaranteed investment contracts
d. Short positions

28. A _____ is a listing of bonds or fixed income instruments and a statistic reflecting the composite value of its components. It is used as a tool to represent the characteristics of its component fixed income instruments. They differ from stock market indices in their complexity.
a. Bond market index
b. 4-4-5 Calendar
c. 7-Eleven
d. 529 plan

29. _____ denotes the total number of derivative contracts, like futures and options, that are currently active on a specific underlying security, having specific terms.

Namely, the total contracts for a specific strike price and expiration date, that have been traded, but have not yet expired, have not yet been closed through a closing transaction, or have not yet been terminated via early exercise. A closing transaction occurs when a counterparty that longs the contract sells, or, conversely, when a counterparty that shorts the contract buys.

a. Equity swap
b. Equity derivative
c. International Swaps and Derivatives Association
d. Open interest

30. _____ is a fee paid on borrowed assets. It is the price paid for the use of borrowed money , or, money earned by deposited funds . Assets that are sometimes lent with _____ include money, shares, consumer goods through hire purchase, major assets such as aircraft, and even entire factories in finance lease arrangements.
a. A Random Walk Down Wall Street
b. Interest
c. AAB
d. Insolvency

31. _____ is the difference between price and the costs of bringing to market whatever it is that is accounted as an enterprise (whether by harvest, extraction, manufacture, or purchase) in terms of the component costs of delivered goods and/or services and any operating or other expenses.

A key difficulty in measuring profit is in defining costs. Pure economic monetary profits can be zero or negative even in competitive equilibrium when accounted monetized costs exceed monetized price.

a. Accounting profit
c. AAB
b. Economic profit
d. A Random Walk Down Wall Street

32. A _____ is a financial contract between two parties, the buyer and the seller of this type of option. Often it is simply labeled a 'call'. The buyer of the option has the right, but not the obligation to buy an agreed quantity of a particular commodity or financial instrument (the underlying instrument) from the seller of the option at a certain time (the expiration date) for a certain price (the strike price.)
   a. Bear spread
   c. Bear call spread
   b. Bull spread
   d. Call option

33. In options, the _____ is a key variable in a derivatives contract between two parties. Where the contract requires delivery of the underlying instrument, the trade will be at the _____, regardless of the spot price (market price) of the underlying instrument at that time.

Definition - The fixed price at which the owner of an option can purchase, in the case of a call in the case of a put, the underlying security or commodity.

   a. Naked put
   c. Moneyness
   b. Swaption
   d. Strike price

34. An _____ is a contract written by a seller that conveys to the buyer the right -- but not the obligation -- to buy (in the case of a call _____) or to sell (in the case of a put _____) a particular asset, such as a piece of property such as, among others, a futures contract. In return for granting the _____, the seller collects a payment (the premium) from the buyer.

For example, buying a call _____ provides the right to buy a specified quantity of a security at a set strike price at some time on or before expiration, while buying a put _____ provides the right to sell.

   a. Option
   c. AT'T Mobility LLC
   b. Annuity
   d. Amortization

35. A _____ is a financial contract between two parties, the seller (writer) and the buyer of the option. The put allows its buyer the right but not the obligation to sell a commodity or financial instrument (the underlying instrument) to the writer (seller) of the option at a certain time for a certain price (the strike price.) The writer (seller) has the obligation to purchase the underlying asset at that strike price, if the buyer exercises the option.
   a. Debit spread
   c. Bear spread
   b. Bear call spread
   d. Put option

36. The term _____ refers to three closely related concepts:

   - The _____ model is a mathematical model of the market for an equity, in which the equity's price is a stochastic process.
   - The _____ PDE is a partial differential equation which (in the model) must be satisfied by the price of a derivative on the equity.
   - The _____ formula is the result obtained by solving the _____ PDE for a European call option.

Chapter 10. Derivative Securities Markets

Fischer Black and Myron Scholes first articulated the _____ formula in their 1973 paper, 'The Pricing of Options and Corporate Liabilities.' The foundation for their research relied on work developed by scholars such as Jack L. Treynor, Paul Samuelson, A. James Boness, Sheen T. Kassouf, and Edward O. Thorp. The fundamental insight of _____ is that the option is implicitly priced if the stock is traded.

Robert C. Merton was the first to publish a paper expanding the mathematical understanding of the options pricing model and coined the term '_____' options pricing model.

a. Modified Internal Rate of Return
b. Stochastic volatility
c. Perpetuity
d. Black-Scholes

37. In finance, _____ refers to the value of a security which is intrinsic to or contained in the security itself. It is also frequently called fundamental value. It is ordinarily calculated by summing the future income generated by the asset, and discounting it to the present value.
   a. Amortization
   b. Intrinsic value
   c. Alpha
   d. Accretion

38. In finance, the value of an option consists of two components, its intrinsic value and its _____. Time value is simply the difference between option value and intrinsic value. _____ is also known as theta, extrinsic value, or instrumental value.
   a. Time value
   b. Conservatism
   c. Global Squeeze
   d. Debt buyer

39. A _____ is a futures contract on a short term interest rate (STIR.) Contracts vary, but are often defined on an interest rate index such as 3-month sterling or US dollar LIBOR.

They are traded across a wide range of currencies, including the G12 country currencies and many others.

   a. Dual currency deposit
   b. Real estate derivatives
   c. Notional amount
   d. Financial Future

40. The _____ Options Exchange is a futures exchange based in London. _____ is now part of NYSE Euronext following its takeover by Euronext in January 2002 and Euronext's merger with New York Stock Exchange in April 2007.

The _____ started life on September 30, 1982, to take advantage of the removal of currency controls in the UK in 1979.

   a. 7-Eleven
   b. 4-4-5 Calendar
   c. 529 plan
   d. LIFFE

41. The _____ started life on September 30, 1982, to take advantage of the removal of currency controls in the UK in 1979. The exchange modelled itself after the Chicago Board of Trade and the Chicago Mercantile Exchange. It initially offered futures contracts and options linked to short term interest rates.

Chapter 10. Derivative Securities Markets

a. 4-4-5 Calendar
b. 529 plan
c. 7-Eleven
d. London International Financial Futures Exchange

42. A _____ is a method of measuring a section of the stock market. Many indices are cited by news or financial services firms and are used to benchmark the performance of portfolios such as mutual funds.
   a. Stop order
   b. Trading curb
   c. Program trading
   d. Stock market index

43. An _____ is the price a borrower pays for the use of money they do not own, and the return a lender receives for deferring the use of funds, by lending it to the borrower. _____s are normally expressed as a percentage rate over the period of one year.

_____s targets are also a vital tool of monetary policy and are used to control variables like investment, inflation, and unemployment.

   a. AAB
   b. Interest rate
   c. A Random Walk Down Wall Street
   d. ABN Amro

44. An _____ is a derivative in which one party exchanges a stream of interest payments for another party's stream of cash flows. _____s can be used by hedgers to manage their fixed or floating assets and liabilities. They can also be used by speculators to replicate unfunded bond exposures to profit from changes in interest rates.
   a. International Swaps and Derivatives Association
   b. Equity swap
   c. Interest rate swap
   d. Implied volatility

45. A _____ is a foreign exchange agreement between two parties to exchange principal and fixed rate interest payments on a loan in one currency for principal and fixed rate interest payments on an equal (regarding net present value) loan in another currency. They are motivated by comparative advantage.
   a. Currency pair
   b. Foreign exchange market
   c. Forex swap
   d. Currency swap

46. _____ is the risk (variability in value) borne by an interest-bearing asset, such as a loan or a bond, due to variability of interest rates. In general, as rates rise, the price of a fixed rate bond will fall, and vice versa. _____ is commonly measured by the bond's duration.
   a. International Fisher effect
   b. Official bank rate
   c. A Random Walk Down Wall Street
   d. Interest rate risk

47. The _____ is a trade organization of participants in the market for over-the-counter derivatives. It is headquartered in New York, and has created a standardized contract (Master Agreement) to enter into derivatives transactions. There are currently two versions of the ISDA Master Agreement: the 1992 edition and the 2002 edition.
   a. Interest rate derivative
   b. Equity swap
   c. Open interest
   d. International Swaps and Derivatives Association

48. _____ is a measurement of corporate or economic size equal to the share price times the number of shares outstanding of a public company. As owning stock represents owning the company, including all its equity, capitalization could represent the public opinion of a company's net worth and is a determining factor in stock valuation. Likewise, the capitalization of stock markets or economic regions may be compared to other economic indicators.

a. Just-in-time
c. Market capitalization
b. Proxy fight
d. Synthetic CDO

49.

A _____ is a type of financial intermediary and a type of bank. Commercial banking is also known as business banking. It is a bank that provides checking accounts, savings accounts, and money market accounts and that accepts time deposits.

a. 4-4-5 Calendar
c. 7-Eleven
b. 529 plan
d. Commercial bank

Chapter 11. Commercial Banks: Industry Overview

1.

A _____ is a type of financial intermediary and a type of bank. Commercial banking is also known as business banking. It is a bank that provides checking accounts, savings accounts, and money market accounts and that accepts time deposits.

- a. 529 plan
- b. 4-4-5 Calendar
- c. 7-Eleven
- d. Commercial bank

2. In business and accounting, _____s are everything of value that is owned by a person or company. The balance sheet of a firm records the monetary value of the _____s owned by the firm. The two major _____ classes are tangible _____s and intangible _____s.
- a. Asset
- b. EBITDA
- c. Income
- d. Accounts payable

3. _____, in bookkeeping, refers to assets, liabilities, income, and expenses recorded on individual pages of the so called book of final entry or ledger. Changes in _____ value are made by chronologically posting debit (DR) and credit (CR) entries to its page. Examples of _____s are cash, _____s receivable, mortgages, loans, land and buildings, common stock, sales, services provided, wages, and payroll overhead.
- a. Account
- b. Option
- c. Alpha
- d. Accretion

4. In the most general sense, a _____ is anything that is a hindrance, or puts individuals at a disadvantage.

Before we discuss the financial terms, we should note that a _____ can also have a much more important slang meaning.

This is best described in an example.

- a. McFadden Act
- b. Liability
- c. Limited liability
- d. Covenant

5. _____, in microeconomics, are the cost advantages that a business obtains due to expansion. _____ may be utilized by any size firm expanding its scale of operation.
- a. Articles of incorporation
- b. Uniform Commercial Code
- c. Employee Retirement Income Security Act
- d. Economies of scale

6. The phrase _____ refers to the aspect of corporate strategy, corporate finance and management dealing with the buying, selling and combining of different companies that can aid, finance, or help a growing company in a given industry grow rapidly without having to create another business entity.

An acquisition, also known as a takeover, is the buying of one company (the 'target') by another. An acquisition may be friendly or hostile.

- a. 4-4-5 Calendar
- b. 529 plan
- c. 7-Eleven
- d. Mergers and acquisitions

Chapter 11. Commercial Banks: Industry Overview

7. The institution most often referenced by the word '_____' is a public or publicly traded _____, the shares of which are traded on a public stock exchange (e.g., the New York Stock Exchange or Nasdaq in the United States) where shares of stock of _____s are bought and sold by and to the general public. Most of the largest businesses in the world are publicly traded _____s. However, the majority of _____s are said to be closely held, privately held or close _____s, meaning that no ready market exists for the trading of shares.

   a. Federal Home Loan Mortgage Corporation   b. Depository Trust Company
   c. Protect   d. Corporation

8. In economics, business, and accounting, a _____ is the value of money that has been used up to produce something, and hence is not available for use anymore. In business, the _____ may be one of acquisition, in which case the amount of money expended to acquire it is counted as _____. In this case, money is the input that is gone in order to acquire the thing.

   a. Sliding scale fees   b. Fixed costs
   c. Cost   d. Marginal cost

9. _____ and the related Fisher's linear discriminant are methods used in statistics and machine learning to find the linear combination of features which best separate two or more classes of objects or events. The resulting combination may be used as a linear classifier, or, more commonly, for dimensionality reduction before later classification.

_____ is closely related to ANOVA (analysis of variance) and regression analysis, which also attempt to express one dependent variable as a linear combination of other features or measurements.

   a. 529 plan   b. 4-4-5 Calendar
   c. Linear discriminant analysis   d. 7-Eleven

10. A _____ or bank is a financial institution whose primary activity is to act as a payment agent for customers and to borrow and lend money.

The first modern bank was founded in Italy in Genoa in 1406, its name was Banco di San Giorgio (Bank of St. George.)

Many other financial activities were added over time.

   a. Black Sea Trade and Development Bank   b. Banker
   c. 4-4-5 Calendar   d. Bought deal

11. _____ is the provision of resources (such as granting a loan) by one party to another party where that second party does not reimburse the first party immediately, thereby generating a debt, and instead arranges either to repay or return those resources (or material(s) of equal value) at a later date. The first party is called a creditor, also known as a lender, while the second party is called a debtor, also known as a borrower.

Movements of financial capital are normally dependent on either _____ or equity transfers.

   a. Comparable   b. Clearing house
   c. Warrant   d. Credit

12. In business, _____ is income that a company receives from its normal business activities, usually from the sale of goods and services to customers. Some companies also receive _____ from interest, dividends or royalties paid to them by other companies. _____ may refer to business income in general, or it may refer to the amount, in a monetary unit, received during a period of time, as in 'Last year, Company X had _____ of $32 million.'

In many countries, including the UK, _____ is referred to as turnover.

  a. Revenue   b. Furniture, Fixtures and Equipment
  c. Matching principle   d. Bottom line

13. In the United States, _____ are overnight borrowings by banks to maintain their bank reserves at the Federal Reserve. Banks keep reserves at Federal Reserve Banks to meet their reserve requirements and to clear financial transactions. Transactions in the _____ market enable depository institutions with reserve balances in excess of reserve requirements to lend reserves to institutions with reserve deficiencies.

  a. Federal funds   b. Regulation T
  c. 4-4-5 Calendar   d. Federal funds rate

14. _____ consists of the sale of goods or merchandise from a fixed location, such as a department store, boutique or kiosk in small or individual lots for direct consumption by the purchaser. _____ may include subordinated services, such as delivery. Purchasers may be individuals or businesses.

  a. 529 plan   b. 7-Eleven
  c. 4-4-5 Calendar   d. Retailing

15. _____ is a fee paid on borrowed assets. It is the price paid for the use of borrowed money , or, money earned by deposited funds . Assets that are sometimes lent with _____ include money, shares, consumer goods through hire purchase, major assets such as aircraft, and even entire factories in finance lease arrangements.

  a. A Random Walk Down Wall Street   b. AAB
  c. Insolvency   d. Interest

16. An _____ is the price a borrower pays for the use of money they do not own, and the return a lender receives for deferring the use of funds, by lending it to the borrower. _____s are normally expressed as a percentage rate over the period of one year.

_____s targets are also a vital tool of monetary policy and are used to control variables like investment, inflation, and unemployment.

  a. ABN Amro   b. AAB
  c. Interest rate   d. A Random Walk Down Wall Street

17. A _____ is a fungible, negotiable instrument representing financial value. They are broadly categorized into debt securities (such as banknotes, bonds and debentures), and equity securities; e.g., common stocks. The company or other entity issuing the _____ is called the issuer.

  a. Book entry   b. Security
  c. Securities lending   d. Tracking stock

18. In finance, a _____ is collateral that the holder of a position in securities, options, or futures contracts has to deposit to cover the credit risk of his counterparty (most often his broker.) This risk can arise if the holder has done any of the following:

- borrowed cash from the counterparty to buy securities or options,
- sold securities or options short, or
- entered into a futures contract.

The collateral can be in the form of cash or securities, and it is deposited in a _____ account. On U.S. futures exchanges, '_____' was formally called performance bond.

_____ buying is buying securities with cash borrowed from a broker, using other securities as collateral.

a. Credit
b. Share
c. Procter ' Gamble
d. Margin

19. _____, refers to consumption opportunity gained by an entity within a specified time frame, which is generally expressed in monetary terms. However, for households and individuals, '_____ is the sum of all the wages, salaries, profits, interests payments, rents and other forms of earnings received... in a given period of time.' For firms, _____ generally refers to net-profit: what remains of revenue after expenses have been subtracted.

a. OIBDA
b. Accrual
c. Annual report
d. Income

20. _____ is the difference between operating revenues and operating expenses, but it is also sometimes used as a synonym for EBIT and operating profit. This is true if the firm has no non-_____.

A professional investor contemplating a change to the capital structure of a firm (e.g., through a leveraged buyout) first evaluates a firm's fundamental earnings potential (reflected by Earnings Before Interest, Taxes, Depreciation and Amortization EBITDA and EBIT), and then determines the optimal use of debt vs. equity.

a. Operating income
b. A Random Walk Down Wall Street
c. ABN Amro
d. AAB

21. The free _____ of a public company is an estimate of the proportion of shares that are not held by large owners and that are not stock with sales restrictions (restricted stock that cannot be sold until they become unrestricted stock.)

The free _____ or a public _____ is usually defined as being all shares held by investors other than:

- shares held by owners owning more than 5% of all shares (those could be institutional investors, 'strategic shareholders,' founders, executives, and other insiders' holdings)
- restricted stocks (granted to executives that can be, but don't have to be, registered insiders)
- insider holdings (it is assumed that insiders hold stock for the very long term)

The free _____ is an important criterion in quoting a share on the stock market.

To _____ a company means to list its shares on a public stock exchange through an initial public offering (or 'flotation'.)

- Open market
- Outstanding shares
- Market capitalization
- Public _____ *loat*
- Reverse takeover

a. Golden parachute   b. Trade finance
c. Synthetic CDO   d. Float

22. _____ (General) is the electronic delivery and presentation of financial statements, bills, invoices, and related information sent by a company to its customers. _____ is also known as other payment models based on consumer-to-business and business-to-business:

- _____PP -- Electronic Bill Presentment ' Payment (typically focused on business-to-consumer billing and payment)
- EIPP -- Electronic Invoice Presentment and Payment (typically focused on business-to-business billing and payment)
- E-commerce payment systems

a. Online accounting   b. Amortization calculator
c. EInvoice   d. Electronic billing

23. _____ refers to the computer-based systems used to perform financial transactions electronically.

The term is used for a number of different concepts:

- Cardholder-initiated transactions, where a cardholder makes use of a payment card
- Direct deposit payroll payments for a business to its employees, possibly via a payroll services company
- Direct debit payments from customer to business, where the transaction is initiated by the business with customer permission
- Electronic bill payment in online banking, which may be delivered by _____ or paper check
- Transactions involving stored value of electronic money, possibly in a private currency
- Wire transfer via an international banking network (generally carries a higher fee)
- Electronic Benefit Transfer

Electronic funds transferPOS (short for _____ at Point of Sale) is an Australian and New Zealand electronic processing system for credit cards, debit cards and charge cards.

European banks and card companies also sometimes reference 'Electronic funds transferPOS' as the system used for processing card transactions through terminals on points of sale, though the system is not the trademarked Australian/New Zealand variant.

Credit cards

_____ may be initiated by a cardholder when a payment card such as a credit card or debit card is used.

a. Electronic funds transfer
c. AAB
b. A Random Walk Down Wall Street
d. ABN Amro

24. A standard, commercial _____ is a document issued mostly by a financial institution, used primarily in trade finance, which usually provides an irrevocable payment undertaking.

The _____ can also be the source of payment for a transaction, meaning that redeeming the _____ will pay an exporter. Letters of credit are used primarily in international trade transactions of significant value, for deals between a supplier in one country and a customer in another.

a. McFadden Act
c. Bond indenture
b. Duty of loyalty
d. Letter of credit

25. A _____ is an option granting its owner the right but not the obligation to enter into an underlying swap. Although options can be traded on a variety of swaps, the term '_____' typically refers to options on interest rate swaps.

There are two types of _____ contracts:

- A payer _____ gives the owner of the _____ the right to enter into a swap where they pay the fixed leg and receive the floating leg.
- A receiver _____ gives the owner of the _____ the right to enter into a swap where they will receive the fixed leg, and pay the floating leg.

The buyer and seller of the _____ agree on:

- the premium (price) of the _____
- the strike rate (equal to the fixed rate of the underlying swap)
- length of the option period (which usually ends two business days prior to the start date of the underlying swap),
- the term of the underlying swap,
- notional amount,
- amortization, if any
- frequency of settlement of payments on the underlying swap

The participants in the _____ market are predominantly large corporations, banks, financial institutions and hedge funds. End users such as corporations and banks typically use _____s to manage interest rate risk arising from their core business or from their financing arrangements.

   a. Bear call spread
   c. Put option
   b. Straddle
   d. Swaption

26. In United States banking, _____ is a marketing term for certain services offered primarily to larger business customers. It may be used to describe all bank accounts (such as checking accounts) provided to businesses of a certain size, but it is more often used to describe specific services such as cash concentration, zero balance accounting, and automated clearing house facilities. Sometimes, private banking customers are given _____ services.

   a. Global tactical asset allocation
   c. Profitability index
   b. Capitalization rate
   d. Cash management

27. _____, consists of the buying and selling of products or services over electronic systems such as the Internet and other computer networks. The amount of trade conducted electronically has grown extraordinarily with widespread Internet usage. The use of commerce is conducted in this way, spurring and drawing on innovations in electronic funds transfer, supply chain management, Internet marketing, online transaction processing, electronic data interchange (EDI), inventory management systems, and automated data collection systems.

   a. A Random Walk Down Wall Street
   c. Electronic commerce
   b. AAB
   d. ABN Amro

28. Explicit _____ is a measure implemented in many countries to protect bank depositors, in full or in part, from losses caused by a bank's inability to pay its debts when due. _____ systems are one component of a financial system safety net that promotes financial stability.

   a. Reserve requirement
   c. Time deposit
   b. Banking panic
   d. Deposit Insurance

29. The _____ is a United States government corporation created by the Glass-Steagall Act of 1933. It provides deposit insurance, which guarantees the safety of checking and savings deposits in member banks, currently up to $250,000 per depositor per bank. Insured deposits are backed by the full faith and credit of the United States.

   a. FASB
   c. NYSE Group
   b. Ford Foundation
   d. Federal Deposit Insurance Corporation

30. _____ is the removal or simplification of government rules and regulations that constrain the operation of market forces. _____ does not mean elimination of laws against fraud, but eliminating or reducing government control of how business is done, thereby moving toward a more free market.

The stated rationale for '_____' is often that fewer and simpler regulations will lead to a raised level of competitiveness, therefore higher productivity, more efficiency and lower prices overall.

   a. Deregulation
   c. Demand shock
   b. Value added
   d. Supply shock

31. In financial accounting, the term _____ is most commonly used to describe any part of shareholders' equity, except for basic share capital. Sometimes, the term is used instead of the term provision; such a use, however, is inconsistent with the terminology suggested by International Accounting Standards Board. For more information about provisions, see provision (accounting.)
   a. Closing entries
   b. Treasury stock
   c. FIFO and LIFO accounting
   d. Reserve

32. A _____ is a company that owns other companies' outstanding stock. It usually refers to a company which does not produce goods or services itself, rather its only purpose is owning shares of other companies. They allow the reduction of risk for the owners and can allow the ownership and control of a number of different companies.
   a. MRU Holdings
   b. Federal National Mortgage Association
   c. Privately held company
   d. Holding company

Chapter 12. Commercial Banks' Financial Statements and Analysis

1. The _____ is a United States government corporation created by the Glass-Steagall Act of 1933. It provides deposit insurance, which guarantees the safety of checking and savings deposits in member banks, currently up to $250,000 per depositor per bank. Insured deposits are backed by the full faith and credit of the United States.
   a. NYSE Group
   b. Ford Foundation
   c. FASB
   d. Federal Deposit Insurance Corporation

2. _____ are formal records of a business' financial activities.

   _____ provide an overview of a business' financial condition in both short and long term. There are four basic _____:

   1. **Balance sheet**: also referred to as statement of financial position or condition, reports on a company's assets, liabilities, and net equity as of a given point in time.
   2. **Income statement**: also referred to as Profit and Loss statement (or a 'P'L'), reports on a company's income, expenses, and profits over a period of time.
   3. **Statement of retained earnings**: explains the changes in a company's retained earnings over the reporting period.
   4. **Statement of cash flows**: reports on a company's cash flow activities, particularly its operating, investing and financing activities.

   a. Notes to the Financial Statements
   b. Statement on Auditing Standards No. 70: Service Organizations
   c. Statement of retained earnings
   d. Financial statements

3. _____ consists of the sale of goods or merchandise from a fixed location, such as a department store, boutique or kiosk in small or individual lots for direct consumption by the purchaser. _____ may include subordinated services, such as delivery. Purchasers may be individuals or businesses.
   a. 7-Eleven
   b. 529 plan
   c. 4-4-5 Calendar
   d. Retailing

4. _____, refers to consumption opportunity gained by an entity within a specified time frame, which is generally expressed in monetary terms. However, for households and individuals, '_____ is the sum of all the wages, salaries, profits, interests payments, rents and other forms of earnings received... in a given period of time.' For firms, _____ generally refers to net-profit: what remains of revenue after expenses have been subtracted.
   a. OIBDA
   b. Annual report
   c. Accrual
   d. Income

5. In business and accounting, _____s are everything of value that is owned by a person or company. The balance sheet of a firm records the monetary value of the _____s owned by the firm. The two major _____ classes are tangible _____s and intangible _____s.
   a. EBITDA
   b. Accounts payable
   c. Income
   d. Asset

6. In financial accounting, a _____ or statement of financial position is a summary of a person's or organization's balances. Assets, liabilities and ownership equity are listed as of a specific date, such as the end of its financial year. A _____ is often described as a snapshot of a company's financial condition.

Chapter 12. Commercial Banks' Financial Statements and Analysis

a. Statement of retained earnings

b. Statement on Auditing Standards No. 70: Service Organizations

c. Financial statements

d. Balance sheet

7.

A _____ is a type of financial intermediary and a type of bank. Commercial banking is also known as business banking. It is a bank that provides checking accounts, savings accounts, and money market accounts and that accepts time deposits.

a. 529 plan

b. 7-Eleven

c. 4-4-5 Calendar

d. Commercial bank

8. A _____ is a fungible, negotiable instrument representing financial value. They are broadly categorized into debt securities (such as banknotes, bonds and debentures), and equity securities; e.g., common stocks. The company or other entity issuing the _____ is called the issuer.

a. Tracking stock

b. Securities lending

c. Book entry

d. Security

9. _____ refers to the likelihood that changes in the business environment adversely affect operating profits or the value of assets in a specific country. For example, financial factors such as currency controls, devaluation or regulatory changes, or stability factors such as mass riots, civil war and other potential events contribute to companies' operational risks. This term is also sometimes referred to as political risk, however _____ is a more general term, which generally only refers to risks affecting all companies operating within a particular country.

a. Solvency

b. Single-index model

c. Capital asset

d. Country risk

10. _____ is the discipline of identifying, monitoring and limiting risks. In some cases the acceptable risk may be near zero. Risks can come from accidents, natural causes and disasters as well as deliberate attacks from an adversary.

a. FIFO

b. Penny stock

c. 4-4-5 Calendar

d. Risk management

11. An _____ is a loan that is not backed by collateral. Also known as a signature loan or personal loan.

_____s are based solely upon the borrower's credit rating.

a. Event of default

b. Annualcreditreport.com

c. Intelliscore

d. Unsecured loan

12. _____, in bookkeeping, refers to assets, liabilities, income, and expenses recorded on individual pages of the so called book of final entry or ledger. Changes in _____ value are made by chronologically posting debit (DR) and credit (CR) entries to its page. Examples of _____s are cash, _____s receivable, mortgages, loans, land and buildings, common stock, sales, services provided, wages, and payroll overhead.

a. Account

b. Alpha

c. Accretion

d. Option

Chapter 12. Commercial Banks' Financial Statements and Analysis

13. In finance, a _____ is a debt security, in which the authorized issuer owes the holders a debt and, depending on the terms of the _____, is obliged to pay interest (the coupon) and/or to repay the principal at a later date, termed maturity.

Thus a _____ is a loan: the issuer is the borrower, the _____ holder is the lender, and the coupon is the interest. _____s provide the borrower with external funds to finance long-term investments, or, in the case of government _____s, to finance current expenditure.

a. Catastrophe bonds
b. Puttable bond
c. Convertible bond
d. Bond

14. _____ is that which is owed; usually referencing assets owed, but the term can cover other obligations. In the case of assets, _____ is a means of using future purchasing power in the present before a summation has been earned. Some companies and corporations use _____ as a part of their overall corporate finance strategy.

a. Partial Payment
b. Debt
c. Credit cycle
d. Cross-collateralization

15. In finance, the _____ is the global financial market for short-term borrowing and lending. It provides short-term liquidity funding for the global financial system. The _____ is where short-term obligations such as Treasury bills, commercial paper and bankers' acceptances are bought and sold.

a. Cramdown
b. Debt-for-equity swap
c. Consumer debt
d. Money market

16. A _____ is a current account at a banking institution that allows money to be deposited and withdrawn by the account holder, with the transactions and resulting balance being recorded on the bank's books. Some banks charge a fee for this service, while others may pay the customer interest on the funds deposited.

Although restrictions placed on access depend upon the terms and conditions of the account and the provider, the account holder retains rights to have their funds repaid on demand.

a. 4-4-5 Calendar
b. Bilateral netting
c. Contractum trinius
d. Deposit account

17. The term _____ describes a reduction in recognized value. In accounting terminology, it refers to recognition of the reduced or zero value of an asset. In income tax statements, it refers to a reduction of taxable income as recognition of certain expenses required to produce the income.

a. Net income
b. Trial balance
c. Net profit
d. Write-off

18. A _____ s a time deposit, a financial product commonly offered to consumers by banks, thrift institutions, and credit unions.

They are similar to savings accounts in that they are insured and thus virtually risk-free; they are 'money in the bank'. They are different from savings accounts in that they have a specific, fixed term (often three months, six months, or one to five years), and, usually, a fixed interest rate.

Chapter 12. Commercial Banks`Financial Statements and Analysis

a. Time deposit
c. Reserve requirement
b. Variable rate mortgage
d. Certificate of deposit

19. _____s are deposits denominated in United States dollars at banks outside the United States, and thus are not under the jurisdiction of the Federal Reserve. Consequently, such deposits are subject to much less regulation than similar deposits within the United States, allowing for higher margins. There is nothing 'European' about _____ deposits; a US dollar-denominated deposit in Tokyo or Caracas would likewise be deemed _____ deposits.
a. Eurodollar
c. A Random Walk Down Wall Street
b. ABN Amro
d. AAB

20. A standard, commercial _____ is a document issued mostly by a financial institution, used primarily in trade finance, which usually provides an irrevocable payment undertaking.

The _____ can also be the source of payment for a transaction, meaning that redeeming the _____ will pay an exporter. Letters of credit are used primarily in international trade transactions of significant value, for deals between a supplier in one country and a customer in another.

a. Bond indenture
c. Letter of credit
b. McFadden Act
d. Duty of loyalty

21. _____ is the provision of resources (such as granting a loan) by one party to another party where that second party does not reimburse the first party immediately, thereby generating a debt, and instead arranges either to repay or return those resources (or material(s) of equal value) at a later date. The first party is called a creditor, also known as a lender, while the second party is called a debtor, also known as a borrower.

Movements of financial capital are normally dependent on either _____ or equity transfers.

a. Clearing house
c. Comparable
b. Warrant
d. Credit

22. A _____ is an exchange of promises between two or more parties to do an act which is enforceable in a court of law. It is where an unqualified offer meets a qualified acceptance and the parties reach Consensus ad Idem. The parties must have the necessary capacity to _____ and the _____ must not be either trifling, indeterminate, impossible or illegal.
a. 4-4-5 Calendar
c. 7-Eleven
b. Contract
d. 529 plan

23. A _____ is a financial contract whose value is derived from the value of something else (known as the underlying.) The underlying on which a _____ is based can be an asset, weather conditions bonds or other forms of credit.
a. 529 plan
c. Derivative
b. 7-Eleven
d. 4-4-5 Calendar

24. An _____ is a financial statement for companies that indicates how Revenue is transformed into net income The purpose of the _____ is to show managers and investors whether the company made or lost money during the period being reported.

Chapter 12. Commercial Banks' Financial Statements and Analysis

The important thing to remember about an _____ is that it represents a period of time.

a. AAB
b. A Random Walk Down Wall Street
c. ABN Amro
d. Income statement

25. _____ is a fee paid on borrowed assets. It is the price paid for the use of borrowed money, or, money earned by deposited funds. Assets that are sometimes lent with _____ include money, shares, consumer goods through hire purchase, major assets such as aircraft, and even entire factories in finance lease arrangements.

a. A Random Walk Down Wall Street
b. Insolvency
c. AAB
d. Interest

26. _____ relates to the cost of borrowing money. It is the price that a lender charges a borrower for the use of the lender's money. _____ is different from OPEX and CAPEX, for it relates to the capital structure of a company.

a. Interest expense
b. A Random Walk Down Wall Street
c. ABN Amro
d. AAB

27. In financial accounting, _____s are precautions for which the amount or probability of occurrence are not known. Typical examples are _____s for warranty costs and _____ for taxes the term reserve is used instead of term _____; such a use, however, is inconsistent with the terminology suggested by International Accounting Standards Board.

a. Momentum Accounting and Triple-Entry Bookkeeping
b. Petty cash
c. Provision
d. Money measurement concept

28. _____ is equal to the income that a firm has after subtracting costs and expenses from the total revenue. _____ can be distributed among holders of common stock as a dividend or held by the firm as retained earnings. _____ is an accounting term; in some countries (such as the UK) profit is the usual term.

a. Net income
b. Write-off
c. Historical cost
d. Furniture, Fixtures and Equipment

29. _____ is the difference between operating revenues and operating expenses, but it is also sometimes used as a synonym for EBIT and operating profit. This is true if the firm has no non-_____.

A professional investor contemplating a change to the capital structure of a firm (e.g., through a leveraged buyout) first evaluates a firm's fundamental earnings potential (reflected by Earnings Before Interest, Taxes, Depreciation and Amortization EBITDA and EBIT), and then determines the optimal use of debt vs. equity.

a. AAB
b. Operating income
c. ABN Amro
d. A Random Walk Down Wall Street

30. _____ measures the rate of return on the ownership interest (shareholders' equity) of the common stock owners. _____ is viewed as one of the most important financial ratios. It measures a firm's efficiency at generating profits from every dollar of shareholders' equity (also known as net assets or assets minus liabilities.)

a. Return on equity   b. Return of capital
c. Diluted Earnings Per Share   d. Return on sales

31. _____ is the difference between price and the costs of bringing to market whatever it is that is accounted as an enterprise (whether by harvest, extraction, manufacture, or purchase) in terms of the component costs of delivered goods and/or services and any operating or other expenses.

A key difficulty in measuring profit is in defining costs. Pure economic monetary profits can be zero or negative even in competitive equilibrium when accounted monetized costs exceed monetized price.

a. AAB   b. Economic profit
c. A Random Walk Down Wall Street   d. Accounting profit

32. _____, Net Margin, Net _____ or Net Profit Ratio all refer to a measure of profitability. It is calculated using a formula and written as a percentage or a number.

$$\text{Net profit margin} = \frac{\text{Net profit after taxes}}{\text{Net Sales}}$$

The _____ is mostly used for internal comparison.

a. 4-4-5 Calendar   b. Profit maximization
c. Net profit margin   d. Profit margin

33. The _____ percentage shows how profitable a company's assets are in generating revenue.

_____ can be computed as:

$$\text{ROA} = \frac{\text{Net Income}}{\text{Total Assets}}$$

This number tells you 'what the company can do with what it's got', i.e. how many dollars of earnings they derive from each dollar of assets they control. It's a useful number for comparing competing companies in the same industry.

a. Return on assets   b. P/E ratio
c. Return on sales   d. Receivables turnover ratio

34. In finance, a _____ is collateral that the holder of a position in securities, options, or futures contracts has to deposit to cover the credit risk of his counterparty (most often his broker.) This risk can arise if the holder has done any of the following:

- borrowed cash from the counterparty to buy securities or options,
- sold securities or options short, or
- entered into a futures contract.

The collateral can be in the form of cash or securities, and it is deposited in a _____ account. On U.S. futures exchanges, '_____' was formally called performance bond.

_____ buying is buying securities with cash borrowed from a broker, using other securities as collateral.

a. Share
b. Credit
c. Procter ' Gamble
d. Margin

Chapter 13. Regulation of Commercial Banks

1. _____ is the provision of resources (such as granting a loan) by one party to another party where that second party does not reimburse the first party immediately, thereby generating a debt, and instead arranges either to repay or return those resources (or material(s) of equal value) at a later date. The first party is called a creditor, also known as a lender, while the second party is called a debtor, also known as a borrower.

Movements of financial capital are normally dependent on either _____ or equity transfers.

   a. Comparable
   b. Warrant
   c. Clearing house
   d. Credit

2. _____ is the process by which the government, or monetary authority of a country controls (i) the supply of money central bank (ii) availability of money, and (iii) cost of money or rate of interest, in order to attain a set of objectives oriented towards the growth and stability of the economy. Monetary theory provides insight into how to craft optimal _____.

_____ is referred to as either being an expansionary policy where an expansionary policy increases the total supply of money in the economy, and a contractionary policy decreases the total money supply.

   a. Federal Open Market Committee
   b. Natural resources consumption tax
   c. Tax exemption
   d. Monetary policy

3. _____ is a United States government regulation that put a limit on the interest rates that banks could pay, including a rate of zero on demand deposits (checking accounts.) Section 11 of the Banking Act of 1933 (12 U.S.C. 371a) prohibits member banks from paying interest on demand deposits, which is implemented by _____
   a. Fair Credit Reporting Act
   b. Regulation Q
   c. Fair Credit Billing Act
   d. Truth in Lending Act

4. The _____ of 1933 established the Federal Deposit Insurance Corporation (FDIC) in the United States and included banking reforms, some of which were designed to control speculation. Some provisions such as Regulation Q, which allowed the Federal Reserve to regulate interest rates in savings accounts, were repealed by the Depository Institutions Deregulation and Monetary Control Act of 1980. Provisions that prohibit a bank holding company from owning other financial companies were repealed on November 12, 1999, by the Gramm-Leach-Bliley Act.
   a. Glass-Steagall Act
   b. 7-Eleven
   c. 529 plan
   d. 4-4-5 Calendar

5. A _____ or bank is a financial institution whose primary activity is to act as a payment agent for customers and to borrow and lend money.

The first modern bank was founded in Italy in Genoa in 1406, its name was Banco di San Giorgio (Bank of St. George.)

Many other financial activities were added over time.

   a. Black Sea Trade and Development Bank
   b. Banker
   c. 4-4-5 Calendar
   d. Bought deal

6. _____ refer to services provided by the finance industry.

The finance industry encompasses a broad range of organizations that deal with the management of money. Among these organizations are banks, credit card companies, insurance companies, consumer finance companies, stock brokerages, investment funds and some government sponsored enterprises.

- a. Financial instruments
- b. Cost of carry
- c. Delta hedging
- d. Financial services

7. A _____ is a company that owns other companies' outstanding stock. It usually refers to a company which does not produce goods or services itself, rather its only purpose is owning shares of other companies. They allow the reduction of risk for the owners and can allow the ownership and control of a number of different companies.
- a. Federal National Mortgage Association
- b. Privately held company
- c. MRU Holdings
- d. Holding company

8. The _____ of 1956 (12 U.S.C. § 1841, et seq.) is a United States Act of Congress that regulates the actions of bank holding companies.

The original law (subsequently amended), specified that the Federal Reserve Board of Governors must approve the establishment of a bank holding company, and prohibited bank holding companies headquartered in one state from acquiring a bank in another state. The law was implemented in part to regulate and control banks that had formed bank holding companies in order to own both banking and non-banking businesses.

- a. Truth in Lending Act
- b. Fair Credit Billing Act
- c. Fair Credit Reporting Act
- d. Bank Holding Company Act

9. The _____ is a United States government corporation created by the Glass-Steagall Act of 1933. It provides deposit insurance, which guarantees the safety of checking and savings deposits in member banks, currently up to $250,000 per depositor per bank. Insured deposits are backed by the full faith and credit of the United States.
- a. Federal Deposit Insurance Corporation
- b. NYSE Group
- c. FASB
- d. Ford Foundation

10. The _____ is a United States federal law enacted in 1927 from recommendations made by the comptroller of the currency Henry May Dawes.

The Act sought to give national banks competitive equality with state-chartered banks by letting national banks branch to the extent permitted by state law. The _____ specifically prohibited interstate branching by allowing each national bank to branch only within the state in which it is situated.

- a. Duty of loyalty
- b. Business valuation
- c. McFadden Act
- d. Covenant

11. A _____, in business matters, is an entity that is controlled by a bigger and more powerful entity. The controlled entity is called a company, corporation, or limited liability company, and the controlling entity is called its parent (or the parent company.) The reason for this distinction is that a lone company cannot be a _____ of any organization; only an entity representing a legal fiction as a separate entity can be a _____.

Chapter 13. Regulation of Commercial Banks

a. 529 plan
b. Subsidiary
c. 4-4-5 Calendar
d. Joint stock company

12. The institution most often referenced by the word '_____' is a public or publicly traded _____, the shares of which are traded on a public stock exchange (e.g., the New York Stock Exchange or Nasdaq in the United States) where shares of stock of _____s are bought and sold by and to the general public. Most of the largest businesses in the world are publicly traded _____s. However, the majority of _____s are said to be closely held, privately held or close _____s, meaning that no ready market exists for the trading of shares.
   a. Depository Trust Company
   b. Protect
   c. Federal Home Loan Mortgage Corporation
   d. Corporation

13. Explicit _____ is a measure implemented in many countries to protect bank depositors, in full or in part, from losses caused by a bank's inability to pay its debts when due. _____ systems are one component of a financial system safety net that promotes financial stability.
   a. Time deposit
   b. Deposit Insurance
   c. Banking panic
   d. Reserve requirement

14. The _____ (FSLIC) was an institution that administered deposit insurance for savings and loan institutions in the United States. It was abolished in 1989 by the Financial Institutions Reform, Recovery and Enforcement Act, which passed responsibility for savings and loan deposit insurance to the Federal Deposit Insurance Corporation (FDIC.)

The FSLIC was created as part of the National Housing Act of 1934 in order to insure deposits in savings and loans, a year after the FDIC was created to insure deposits in commercial banks.

   a. Prudent man rule
   b. Securities Investor Protection Corporation
   c. Federal Savings and Loan Insurance Corporation
   d. SIPC

15. In financial accounting, a _____ or statement of financial position is a summary of a person's or organization's balances. Assets, liabilities and ownership equity are listed as of a specific date, such as the end of its financial year. A _____ is often described as a snapshot of a company's financial condition.
   a. Statement on Auditing Standards No. 70: Service Organizations
   b. Financial statements
   c. Statement of retained earnings
   d. Balance sheet

16.

A _____ is a type of financial intermediary and a type of bank. Commercial banking is also known as business banking. It is a bank that provides checking accounts, savings accounts, and money market accounts and that accepts time deposits.

   a. 4-4-5 Calendar
   b. 529 plan
   c. 7-Eleven
   d. Commercial bank

17. _____ is a measure of the ability of a debtor to pay their debts as and when they fall due. It is usually expressed as a ratio or a percentage of current liabilities.

Chapter 13. Regulation of Commercial Banks

For a corporation with a published balance sheet there are various ratios used to calculate a measure of liquidity.

a. Accounting liquidity
b. Invested capital
c. Operating leverage
d. Operating profit margin

18. In finance, _____ (or gearing) is borrowing money to supplement existing funds for investment in such a way that the potential positive or negative outcome is magnified and/or enhanced. It generally refers to using borrowed funds, or debt, so as to attempt to increase the returns to equity. Deleveraging is the action of reducing borrowings.

a. Limited partnership
b. Financial endowment
c. Pension fund
d. Leverage

19. _____ is a type of trade policy that allows traders to act and transact without interference from government. Thus, the policy permits trading partners mutual gains from trade, with goods and services produced according to the theory of comparative advantage.

Under a _____ policy, prices are a reflection of true supply and demand, and are the sole determinant of resource allocation.

a. Monte Carlo methods
b. Seasoned equity offering
c. Yield spread
d. Free Trade

20. The _____ is a trilateral trade bloc in North America created by the governments of the United States, Canada, and Mexico. The agreement creating the trade bloc came into force on January 1, 1994. It superseded the Canada-United States Free Trade Agreement between the U.S. and Canada.

a. 4-4-5 Calendar
b. 7-Eleven
c. 529 plan
d. North American Free Trade Agreement

21. In financial accounting, the term _____ is most commonly used to describe any part of shareholders' equity, except for basic share capital. Sometimes, the term is used instead of the term provision; such a use, however, is inconsistent with the terminology suggested by International Accounting Standards Board. For more information about provisions, see provision (accounting.)

a. Closing entries
b. Treasury stock
c. Reserve
d. FIFO and LIFO accounting

Chapter 14. Other Lending Institutions: Savings Institutions, Credit Unions

1. The U.S. _____ is an independent agency of the United States government which holds primary responsibility for enforcing the federal securities laws and regulating the securities industry, the nation's stock and options exchanges, and other electronic securities markets. The SEC was created by section 4 of the SEC of 1934 (now codified as 15 U.S.C. § 78d and commonly referred to as the 1934 Act.)
   - a. 7-Eleven
   - b. 4-4-5 Calendar
   - c. Securities and Exchange Commission
   - d. 529 plan

2. _____ is the discipline of identifying, monitoring and limiting risks. In some cases the acceptable risk may be near zero. Risks can come from accidents, natural causes and disasters as well as deliberate attacks from an adversary.
   - a. 4-4-5 Calendar
   - b. FIFO
   - c. Penny stock
   - d. Risk management

3. A _____ is a financial institution that specializes in accepting savings deposits and making mortgage and other loans. The S'L or thrift term is mainly used in the United States; similar institutions in the United Kingdom, Ireland and some Commonwealth countries include building societies and trustee savings banks.

   They are often mutually held, meaning that the depositors and borrowers are members with voting rights, and have the ability to direct the financial and managerial goals of the organization, not unlike the poliyholders of a mutual insurance company.

   - a. Net asset value
   - b. Mutual fund
   - c. Person-to-person lending
   - d. Savings and loan association

4. In economics, _____ is the removal of intermediaries in a supply chain: 'cutting out the middleman'. Instead of going through traditional distribution channels, which had some type of intermediate (such as a distributor, wholesaler, broker, or agent), companies may now deal with every customer directly, for example via the Internet. One important factor is a drop in the cost of servicing customers directly.
   - a. Disintermediation
   - b. 4-4-5 Calendar
   - c. 7-Eleven
   - d. 529 plan

5. _____ is a United States government regulation that put a limit on the interest rates that banks could pay, including a rate of zero on demand deposits (checking accounts.) Section 11 of the Banking Act of 1933 (12 U.S.C. 371a) prohibits member banks from paying interest on demand deposits, which is implemented by _____
   - a. Regulation Q
   - b. Truth in Lending Act
   - c. Fair Credit Billing Act
   - d. Fair Credit Reporting Act

6. In finance, a _____ is collateral that the holder of a position in securities, options, or futures contracts has to deposit to cover the credit risk of his counterparty (most often his broker.) This risk can arise if the holder has done any of the following:

   - borrowed cash from the counterparty to buy securities or options,
   - sold securities or options short, or
   - entered into a futures contract.

   The collateral can be in the form of cash or securities, and it is deposited in a _____ account. On U.S. futures exchanges, '_____' was formally called performance bond.

Chapter 14. Other Lending Institutions: Savings Institutions, Credit Unions

_____ buying is buying securities with cash borrowed from a broker, using other securities as collateral.

a. Margin
b. Credit
c. Procter ' Gamble
d. Share

7. The institution most often referenced by the word '_____' is a public or publicly traded _____, the shares of which are traded on a public stock exchange (e.g., the New York Stock Exchange or Nasdaq in the United States) where shares of stock of _____s are bought and sold by and to the general public. Most of the largest businesses in the world are publicly traded _____s. However, the majority of _____s are said to be closely held, privately held or close _____s, meaning that no ready market exists for the trading of shares.

a. Protect
b. Federal Home Loan Mortgage Corporation
c. Corporation
d. Depository Trust Company

8. The _____ provide stable, on-demand, low-cost funding to American financial institutions for home mortgage loans, small business, rural, agricultural, and economic development lending. With their members, the _____ank System represents the largest collective source of home mortgage and community credit in the United States. The banks do not provide loans directly to individuals, only to other banks.

a. 7-Eleven
b. 529 plan
c. Federal Home Loan Banks
d. 4-4-5 Calendar

9. The _____, an agency of the United States Department of the Treasury, is the primary regulator of federal savings associations (sometimes referred to as federal thrifts.) Federal savings associations include both federal savings banks and federal savings and loans. The OTS is also responsible for supervising savings and loan holding companies (SLHCs) and some state-chartered institutions.

a. ABN Amro
b. AAB
c. Office of Thrift Supervision
d. A Random Walk Down Wall Street

10. _____ is the provision of resources (such as granting a loan) by one party to another party where that second party does not reimburse the first party immediately, thereby generating a debt, and instead arranges either to repay or return those resources (or material(s) of equal value) at a later date. The first party is called a creditor, also known as a lender, while the second party is called a debtor, also known as a borrower.

Movements of financial capital are normally dependent on either _____ or equity transfers.

a. Clearing house
b. Comparable
c. Warrant
d. Credit

11. A _____ is a cooperative financial institution that is owned and controlled by its members, and operated for the purpose of promoting thrift, providing credit at reasonable rates, and providing other financial services to its members. Many _____s exist to further community development or sustainable international development on a local level. Worldwide, _____ systems vary significantly in terms of total system assets and average institution asset size since _____s exist in a wide range of sizes, ranging from volunteer operations with a handful of members to institutions with several billion dollars in assets and hundreds of thousands of members.

a. Corporate credit union
c. Fi-linx
b. Credit Union Service Organization
d. Credit union

12. _____, in bookkeeping, refers to assets, liabilities, income, and expenses recorded on individual pages of the so called book of final entry or ledger. Changes in _____ value are made by chronologically posting debit (DR) and credit (CR) entries to its page. Examples of _____s are cash, _____s receivable, mortgages, loans, land and buildings, common stock, sales, services provided, wages, and payroll overhead.
   a. Alpha
   b. Account
   c. Accretion
   d. Option

13. In business and finance, a _____ (also referred to as equity _____) of stock means a _____ of ownership in a corporation (company.) In the plural, stocks is often used as a synonym for _____s especially in the United States, but it is less commonly used that way outside of North America.

In the United Kingdom, South Africa, and Australia, stock can also refer to completely different financial instruments such as government bonds or, less commonly, to all kinds of marketable securities.

   a. Margin
   b. Bucket shop
   c. Procter ' Gamble
   d. Share

14. A _____ is a loan made using real estate as collateral to secure repayment.

A _____ is similar to a residential mortgage, except the collateral is a commercial building or other business real estate, not residential property.

In addition, _____s are typically taken on by businesses instead of individual borrowers.

   a. Chain of Blame
   b. Commercial Mortgage
   c. Shared appreciation mortgage
   d. Fixed rate mortgage

15. _____ is a financial transaction whereby a business sells its accounts receivable (i.e., invoices) at a discount. _____ differs from a bank loan in three main ways. First, the emphasis is on the value of the receivables (essentially a financial asset), not the firm's credit worthiness.
   a. Debt-for-equity swap
   b. Factoring
   c. Credit card balance transfer
   d. Financial Literacy Month

16. _____ is one of a series of accounting transactions dealing with the billing of customers who owe money to a person, company or organization for goods and services that have been provided to the customer. In most business entities this is typically done by generating an invoice and mailing or electronically delivering it to the customer, who in turn must pay it within an established timeframe called credit or payment terms.

An example of a common payment term is Net 30, meaning payment is due in the amount of the invoice 30 days from the date of invoice.

Chapter 14. Other Lending Institutions: Savings Institutions, Credit Unions

a. Accounting methods
b. Income
c. Impaired asset
d. Accounts receivable

17. _____ is a structured finance process that involves pooling and repackaging of cash-flow-producing financial assets into securities, which are then sold to investors. The term '_____' is derived from the fact that the form of financial instruments used to obtain funds from the investors are securities. As a portfolio risk backed by amortizing cash flows - and unlike general corporate debt - the credit quality of securitized debt is non-stationary due to changes in volatility that are time- and structure-dependent.

a. Reputational risk
b. Special journals
c. The Glass-Steagall Act of 1933
d. Securitization

18. _____ is the value of a homeowner's unencumbered interest in their property, i.e. the difference between the home's fair market value and the unpaid balance of the mortgage and any outstanding debt over the home. _____ increases as the mortgage is paid or as the property enjoys appreciation. This is sometimes called real property value in economics.

a. Real Estate Investment Trust
b. REIT
c. Liquidation value
d. Home equity

19. In business and accounting, _____s are everything of value that is owned by a person or company. The balance sheet of a firm records the monetary value of the _____s owned by the firm. The two major _____ classes are tangible _____s and intangible _____s.

a. Accounts payable
b. Asset
c. EBITDA
d. Income

20. _____ is a process by which a firm can obtain the use of a certain fixed assets for which it must pay a series of contractual, periodic, tax deductable payments. The lessee is the receiver of the services or the assets under the lease contract and the lessor is the owner of the assets. The relationship between the tenant and the landlord is called a tenancy, and can be for a fixed or an indefinite period of time (called the term of the lease).

a. Quiet period
b. Foreign Corrupt Practices Act
c. Royalties
d. Leasing

Chapter 15. Insurance Companies

1. _____ is the provision of resources (such as granting a loan) by one party to another party where that second party does not reimburse the first party immediately, thereby generating a debt, and instead arranges either to repay or return those resources (or material(s) of equal value) at a later date. The first party is called a creditor, also known as a lender, while the second party is called a debtor, also known as a borrower.

Movements of financial capital are normally dependent on either _____ or equity transfers.

   a. Clearing house
   b. Credit
   c. Comparable
   d. Warrant

2. Credit insurance is a term used to describe both trade credit insurance and _____.

   _____ is a consumer purchase, often sold with a big ticket purchase such as an automobile. The insurance will pay off the loan balance in the event of the death or the disability of the borrower.

   a. 4-4-5 Calendar
   b. Credit life insurance
   c. 7-Eleven
   d. 529 plan

3. _____ or term assurance is life insurance which provides coverage for a limited period of time, the relevant term. After that period, the insured can either drop the policy or pay annually increasing premiums to continue the coverage. If the insured dies during the term, the death benefit will be paid to the beneficiary.
   a. Whole life insurance
   b. Term life insurance
   c. 529 plan
   d. 4-4-5 Calendar

4. _____ is a type of permanent life insurance based on a cash value. That is, the policy is established with the insurer where premium payments above the cost of insurance are credited to the cash value. The cash value is credited each month with interest, and the policy is debited each month by a cost of insurance (COI) charge, and any other policy charges and fees which are drawn from the cash value if no premium payment is made that month.
   a. Universal life
   b. A Random Walk Down Wall Street
   c. ABN Amro
   d. AAB

5. A _____ refers to any type debt instrument, such as a loan, bond, mortgage that does not have a fixed rate of interest over the life of the instrument. Such debt typically uses an index or other base rate for establishing the interest rate for each relevant period. One of the most common rates to use as the basis for applying interest rates is the London Inter-bank Offered Rate, or LIBOR
   a. Cost of living
   b. Disposal tax effect
   c. Foreign exchange hedge
   d. Floating interest rate

6. _____ is a life insurance policy that remains in force for the insured's whole life and requires (in most cases) premiums to be paid every year into the policy.

All life insurance was originally term insurance. However, because term life insurance only pays a claim upon death within the stated term, most term insurance policy holders became upset over the idea that they could be paying premiums for 20 or 30 years and then wind up with nothing to show for it.

Chapter 15. Insurance Companies

  a. 529 plan
  b. 4-4-5 Calendar
  c. Whole life insurance
  d. Term life insurance

7. In finance, a _____ is a debt security, in which the authorized issuer owes the holders a debt and, depending on the terms of the _____, is obliged to pay interest (the coupon) and/or to repay the principal at a later date, termed maturity.

Thus a _____ is a loan: the issuer is the borrower, the _____ holder is the lender, and the coupon is the interest. _____s provide the borrower with external funds to finance long-term investments, or, in the case of government _____s, to finance current expenditure.

  a. Catastrophe bonds
  b. Puttable bond
  c. Bond
  d. Convertible bond

8. In business and accounting, _____s are everything of value that is owned by a person or company. The balance sheet of a firm records the monetary value of the _____s owned by the firm. The two major _____ classes are tangible _____s and intangible _____s.
  a. Accounts payable
  b. Asset
  c. Income
  d. EBITDA

9. In financial accounting, a _____ or statement of financial position is a summary of a person's or organization's balances. Assets, liabilities and ownership equity are listed as of a specific date, such as the end of its financial year. A _____ is often described as a snapshot of a company's financial condition.
  a. Statement on Auditing Standards No. 70: Service Organizations
  b. Financial statements
  c. Balance sheet
  d. Statement of retained earnings

10. _____, in bookkeeping, refers to assets, liabilities, income, and expenses recorded on individual pages of the so called book of final entry or ledger. Changes in _____ value are made by chronologically posting debit (DR) and credit (CR) entries to its page. Examples of _____s are cash, _____s receivable, mortgages, loans, land and buildings, common stock, sales, services provided, wages, and payroll overhead.
  a. Option
  b. Accretion
  c. Alpha
  d. Account

11. In financial accounting, the term _____ is most commonly used to describe any part of shareholders' equity, except for basic share capital. Sometimes, the term is used instead of the term provision; such a use, however, is inconsistent with the terminology suggested by International Accounting Standards Board. For more information about provisions, see provision (accounting.)
  a. Closing entries
  b. Treasury stock
  c. Reserve
  d. FIFO and LIFO accounting

12. In the most general sense, a _____ is anything that is a hindrance, or puts individuals at a disadvantage.

Before we discuss the financial terms, we should note that a _____ can also have a much more important slang meaning.

Chapter 15. Insurance Companies

This is best described in an example.

a. Covenant
b. Limited liability
c. McFadden Act
d. Liability

13. In economic models, the _____ time frame assumes no fixed factors of production. Firms can enter or leave the marketplace, and the cost (and availability) of land, labor, raw materials, and capital goods can be assumed to vary. In contrast, in the short-run time frame, certain factors are assumed to be fixed, because there is not sufficient time for them to change.

a. Long-run
b. Short-run
c. 529 plan
d. 4-4-5 Calendar

14. _____ means regulating, adapting or settling in a variety of contexts:

In commercial law, _____ means the settlement of a loss incurred on insured goods. The calculation of the amounts of compensation to be paid by or to the several interests is a complicated matter. It involves much detail and arithmetic, and requires a full and accurate knowledge of the principles of the subject.

a. Asset recovery
b. Intelligent investor
c. Equity method
d. Adjustment

15. The _____ is a financial term defined as a company's operating expenses as a percentage of revenue. This financial ratio is most commonly used for industries such as railroads which require a large percentage of revenues to maintain operations. In railroading, an _____ of 80 or lower is considered desirable.

a. Underwriting contract
b. Internal financing
c. Employee stock option
d. Operating ratio

16. _____ is the price at which an asset would trade in a competitive Walrasian auction setting. _____ is often used interchangeably with open _____, fair value or fair _____, although these terms have distinct definitions in different standards, and may differ in some circumstances.

International Valuation Standards defines _____ as 'the estimated amount for which a property should exchange on the date of valuation between a willing buyer and a willing seller in an arm'e;s-length transaction after proper marketing wherein the parties had each acted knowledgeably, prudently, and without compulsion.'

_____ is a concept distinct from market price, which is 'e;the price at which one can transact'e;, while _____ is 'e;the true underlying value'e; according to theoretical standards.

a. Wrap account
b. Debt restructuring
c. T-Model
d. Market value

Chapter 16. Securities Firms and Investment Banks

1. The phrase _____ refers to the aspect of corporate strategy, corporate finance and management dealing with the buying, selling and combining of different companies that can aid, finance, or help a growing company in a given industry grow rapidly without having to create another business entity.

An acquisition, also known as a takeover, is the buying of one company (the 'target') by another. An acquisition may be friendly or hostile.

   a. 4-4-5 Calendar   b. 7-Eleven
   c. Mergers and acquisitions   d. 529 plan

2. _____ is the discipline of identifying, monitoring and limiting risks. In some cases the acceptable risk may be near zero. Risks can come from accidents, natural causes and disasters as well as deliberate attacks from an adversary.

   a. Risk management   b. FIFO
   c. 4-4-5 Calendar   d. Penny stock

3. A _____ is a fungible, negotiable instrument representing financial value. They are broadly categorized into debt securities (such as banknotes, bonds and debentures), and equity securities; e.g., common stocks. The company or other entity issuing the _____ is called the issuer.

   a. Securities lending   b. Book entry
   c. Tracking stock   d. Security

4. _____ is the provision of resources (such as granting a loan) by one party to another party where that second party does not reimburse the first party immediately, thereby generating a debt, and instead arranges either to repay or return those resources (or material(s) of equal value) at a later date. The first party is called a creditor, also known as a lender, while the second party is called a debtor, also known as a borrower.

Movements of financial capital are normally dependent on either _____ or equity transfers.

   a. Warrant   b. Credit
   c. Clearing house   d. Comparable

5. A _____ is a company or other organization that trades securities for its own account or on behalf of its customers.

When executing trade orders on behalf of a customer, the institution is said to be acting as a broker. When executing trades for its own account, the institution is said to be acting as a 'dealer.' Securities bought from clients or other firms in the capacity of dealer may be sold to clients or other firms acting again in the capacity of dealer, or they may become a part of the firm's holdings.

   a. Broker-dealer   b. Person-to-person lending
   c. Mutual fund   d. Trust company

6. A '_____' is a 'Charge' that is paid to obtain the right to delay a payment. Essentially, the payer purchases the right to make a given payment in the future instead of in the Present. The '_____', or 'Charge' that must be paid to delay the payment, is simply the difference between what the payment amount would be if it were paid in the present and what the payment amount would be paid if it were paid in the future.

Chapter 16. Securities Firms and Investment Banks

a. Risk aversion
c. Risk modeling
b. Discount
d. Value at risk

7. In the United States, a _____ is an offering of securities that are not registered with the Securities and Exchange Commission (SEC.) Such offerings exploit an exemption offered by the Securities Act of 1933 that comes with several restrictions, including a prohibition against general solicitation. This exemption allows companies to avoid quarterly reporting requirements and many of the legal liabilities associated with the Sarbanes-Oxley Act.
   a. 4-4-5 Calendar
   c. Private placement
   b. 7-Eleven
   d. 529 plan

8. _____ is a type of private equity capital typically provided to early-stage, high-potential, growth companies in the interest of generating a return through an eventual realization event such as an IPO or trade sale of the company. _____ investments are generally made as cash in exchange for shares in the invested company. It is typical for _____ investors to identify and back companies in high technology industries such as biotechnology and ICT.
   a. Probability distribution
   c. Treasury Inflation-Protected Securities
   b. Tail risk
   d. Venture capital

9. The _____ is a federally mandated non-profit corporation in the United States that protects securities investors from harm if a broker-dealer company fails. Investors are not insured for any potential loss while invested in the market.

Congress created _____ in 1970 through the _____ (15 U.S.C.

   a. Prudent man rule
   c. SIPC
   b. Williams Act
   d. Rule 144A

10. In economics and finance, _____ is the practice of taking advantage of a price differential between two or more markets: striking a combination of matching deals that capitalize upon the imbalance, the profit being the difference between the market prices. When used by academics, an _____ is a transaction that involves no negative cash flow at any probabilistic or temporal state and a positive cash flow in at least one state; in simple terms, a risk-free profit.
    a. Efficient-market hypothesis
    c. Initial margin
    b. Issuer
    d. Arbitrage

11. _____ is casually defined as the use of computers in stock markets to engage in arbitrage and portfolio insurance strategies. However, the New York Stock Exchange (NYSE) defines the term as 'a wide range of portfolio trading strategies involving the purchase or sale of 15 or more stocks having a total market value of $1 million or more' without any direct reference to the use of computers. The word 'program' can be interpreted in its earlier, more general meaning of a defined and pre-arranged sequence of steps, rather than specifically a computer program.
    a. Program trading
    c. Wash sale
    b. Share price
    d. Stop order

12. In United States banking, _____ is a marketing term for certain services offered primarily to larger business customers. It may be used to describe all bank accounts (such as checking accounts) provided to businesses of a certain size, but it is more often used to describe specific services such as cash concentration, zero balance accounting, and automated clearing house facilities. Sometimes, private banking customers are given _____ services.

a. Capitalization rate
b. Profitability index
c. Cash management
d. Global tactical asset allocation

13. _____, in bookkeeping, refers to assets, liabilities, income, and expenses recorded on individual pages of the so called book of final entry or ledger. Changes in _____ value are made by chronologically posting debit (DR) and credit (CR) entries to its page. Examples of _____s are cash, _____s receivable, mortgages, loans, land and buildings, common stock, sales, services provided, wages, and payroll overhead.
 a. Accretion
 b. Option
 c. Account
 d. Alpha

14. In financial accounting, a _____ or statement of financial position is a summary of a person's or organization's balances. Assets, liabilities and ownership equity are listed as of a specific date, such as the end of its financial year. A _____ is often described as a snapshot of a company's financial condition.
 a. Financial statements
 b. Statement on Auditing Standards No. 70: Service Organizations
 c. Statement of retained earnings
 d. Balance sheet

15. The _____ of 2002 (Pub.L. 107-204, 116 Stat. 745, enacted July 30, 2002), also known as the Public Company Accounting Reform and Investor Protection Act of 2002 and commonly called Sarbanes-Oxley, Sarbox or SOX, is a United States federal law enacted on July 30, 2002 in response to a number of major corporate and accounting scandals including those affecting Enron, Tyco International, Adelphia, Peregrine Systems and WorldCom.
 a. Duty of loyalty
 b. Foreign Corrupt Practices Act
 c. Blue sky law
 d. Sarbanes-Oxley Act

16. _____, adopted pursuant to the U.S. Securities Act of 1933, as amended (the 'Securities Act') provides a safe harbor from the registration requirements of the Securities Act of 1933 for certain private resales of restricted securities to QIBs (qualified institutional buyers), which generally are large institutional investors with over $100 million in investable assets. When a broker or dealer is selling securities in reliance on _____, it is subject to the condition that it may not make offers to persons other than those it reasonably believes to be QIBs.

Since its adoption, _____ has greatly increased the liquidity of the securities affected.

 a. Rule 144A
 b. SIPC
 c. Prudent man rule
 d. Securities Investor Protection Corporation

17. The U.S. _____ is an independent agency of the United States government which holds primary responsibility for enforcing the federal securities laws and regulating the securities industry, the nation's stock and options exchanges, and other electronic securities markets. The SEC was created by section 4 of the SEC of 1934 (now codified as 15 U.S.C. § 78d and commonly referred to as the 1934 Act.)
 a. 7-Eleven
 b. Securities and Exchange Commission
 c. 4-4-5 Calendar
 d. 529 plan

18. The institution most often referenced by the word '_____' is a public or publicly traded _____, the shares of which are traded on a public stock exchange (e.g., the New York Stock Exchange or Nasdaq in the United States) where shares of stock of _____s are bought and sold by and to the general public. Most of the largest businesses in the world are publicly traded _____s. However, the majority of _____s are said to be closely held, privately held or close _____s, meaning that no ready market exists for the trading of shares.

   a. Depository Trust Company
   b. Protect
   c. Federal Home Loan Mortgage Corporation
   d. Corporation

19. The _____ is a federally mandated non-profit corporation in the United States that protects securities investors from harm if a broker-dealer company fails. Investors are not insured for any potential loss while invested in the market.

Congress created _____ in 1970 through the Securities Investor Protection Act (15 U.S.C.

   a. Rule 144A
   b. SIPC
   c. Prudent man rule
   d. Securities Investor Protection Corporation

20. _____ is an arrangement with the U.S. Securities and Exchange Commission that allows a single registration document to be filed that permits the issuance of multiple securities.

_____ is a registration of a new issue which can be prepared up to two years in advance, so that the issue can be offered quickly as soon as funds are needed or market conditions are favorable.

For example, current market conditions in the housing market are not favorable for a specific firm to issue a public offering.

   a. Shelf registration
   b. 4-4-5 Calendar
   c. Bought deal
   d. Black Sea Trade and Development Bank

Chapter 17. Mutual Funds

1. A _____ is a professionally managed type of collective investment scheme that pools money from many investors and invests it in stocks, bonds, short-term money market instruments, and/or other securities. The _____ will have a fund manager that trades the pooled money on a regular basis. Currently, the worldwide value of all _____s totals more than $26 trillion.

Since 1940, there have been three basic types of investment companies in the United States: open-end funds, also known in the US as _____s; unit investment trusts (UITs); and closed-end funds.

   a. Trust company
   b. Net asset value
   c. Financial intermediary
   d. Mutual fund

2. In finance, a _____ is a debt security, in which the authorized issuer owes the holders a debt and, depending on the terms of the _____, is obliged to pay interest (the coupon) and/or to repay the principal at a later date, termed maturity.

Thus a _____ is a loan: the issuer is the borrower, the _____ holder is the lender, and the coupon is the interest. _____s provide the borrower with external funds to finance long-term investments, or, in the case of government _____s, to finance current expenditure.

   a. Puttable bond
   b. Catastrophe bonds
   c. Bond
   d. Convertible bond

3. A _____ is a collective investment scheme that invests in bonds and other debt securities. _____s yield monthly dividends that include interest payments on the fund's underlying securities plus any capital appreciation in the prices of the portfolio's bonds. _____s tend to pay higher dividends than CDs and money market accounts, and they generally pay out dividends more frequently and regularly than individual bonds.
   a. Bond fund
   b. Gilts
   c. Premium bond
   d. Private activity bond

4. A _____ or equity fund is a fund that invests in Equities more commonly known as stocks. Such funds are typically held either in stock or cash, as opposed to Bonds, notes, or other securities. This may be a mutual fund or exchange-traded fund.
   a. Closed-end fund
   b. Mutual fund fees and expenses
   c. Money market funds
   d. Stock fund

5. In finance, the _____ is the global financial market for short-term borrowing and lending. It provides short-term liquidity funding for the global financial system. The _____ is where short-term obligations such as Treasury bills, commercial paper and bankers' acceptances are bought and sold.
   a. Consumer debt
   b. Debt-for-equity swap
   c. Cramdown
   d. Money market

6. The U.S. _____ is an independent agency of the United States government which holds primary responsibility for enforcing the federal securities laws and regulating the securities industry, the nation's stock and options exchanges, and other electronic securities markets. The SEC was created by section 4 of the SEC of 1934 (now codified as 15 U.S.C. Â§ 78d and commonly referred to as the 1934 Act.)

a. 4-4-5 Calendar
c. 7-Eleven
b. Securities and Exchange Commission
d. 529 plan

7. An _____ is an investment vehicle traded on stock exchanges, much like stocks. An ETF holds assets such as stocks or bonds and trades at approximately the same price as the net asset value of its underlying assets over the course of the trading day. Most ETFs track an index, such as the Dow Jones Industrial Average or the S'P 500.
   a. ABN Amro
   c. A Random Walk Down Wall Street
   b. AAB
   d. Exchange-traded fund

8. An _____ or index tracker is a collective investment scheme (usually a mutual fund or exchange-traded fund) that aims to replicate the movements of an index of a specific financial market regardless of market conditions.

Tracking can be achieved by trying to hold all of the securities in the index, in the same proportions as the index. Other methods include statistically sampling the market and holding 'representative' securities.

   a. Investment company
   c. A Random Walk Down Wall Street
   b. AAB
   d. Index fund

9. _____ is a term used in accounting relating to the increase in value of an asset. In this sense it is the reverse of depreciation, which measures the fall in value of assets over their normal life-time.

_____ is a rise of a currency in a floating exchange rate.

   a. A Random Walk Down Wall Street
   c. Other Comprehensive Basis of Accounting
   b. Operating cash flow
   d. Appreciation

10. A _____ is a pool of assets forming an independent legal entity that are bought with the contributions to a pension plan for the exclusive purpose of financing pension plan benefits.

_____s are important shareholders of listed and private companies. They are especially important to the stock market where large institutional investors like the Ontario Teachers' Pension Plan dominate.

   a. Leverage
   c. Limited liability company
   b. Leveraged buyout
   d. Pension fund

11. A _____ is a fungible, negotiable instrument representing financial value. They are broadly categorized into debt securities (such as banknotes, bonds and debentures), and equity securities; e.g., common stocks. The company or other entity issuing the _____ is called the issuer.
   a. Tracking stock
   c. Security
   b. Book entry
   d. Securities lending

12. A _____ is a financial contract whose value is derived from the value of something else (known as the underlying.) The underlying on which a _____ is based can be an asset, weather conditions bonds or other forms of credit.

a. 4-4-5 Calendar
c. 7-Eleven
b. 529 plan
d. Derivative

13. _____ or fair value accounting refers to the accounting standards of assigning a value to a position held in a financial instrument based on the current fair market price for the instrument or similar instruments. Fair value accounting has been a part of US Generally Accepted Accounting Principles (GAAP) since the early 1990s. The use of fair value measurements has increased steadily over the past decade, primarily in response to investor demand for relevant and timely financial statements that will aid in making better informed decisions.
   a. 529 plan
   c. 7-Eleven
   b. 4-4-5 Calendar
   d. Mark-to-market

14. _____ is a term used to describe the value of an entity's assets less the value of its liabilities. The term is commonly used in relation to collective investment schemes. It may also be used as a synonym for the book value of a firm.
   a. Net asset value
   c. Financial intermediary
   b. Passive management
   d. Retail broker

15. In business and accounting, _____s are everything of value that is owned by a person or company. The balance sheet of a firm records the monetary value of the _____s owned by the firm. The two major _____ classes are tangible _____s and intangible _____s.
   a. Income
   c. Accounts payable
   b. EBITDA
   d. Asset

16. A _____ is a tax designation for a corporation investing in real estate that reduces or eliminates corporate income taxes. In return, _____s are required to distribute 95% of their income, which may be taxable in the hands of the investors. The _____ structure was designed to provide a similar structure for investment in real estate as mutual funds provide for investment in stocks.
   a. Real Estate Investment Trust
   c. Liquidation value
   b. Real estate investing
   d. REIT

17. A _____ or _____ is a tax designation for a corporation investing in real estate that reduces or eliminates corporate income taxes. In return, _____s are required to distribute 95% of their income, which may be taxable in the hands of the investors. The _____ structure was designed to provide a similar structure for investment in real estate as mutual funds provide for investment in stocks.
   a. Tenancy
   c. Liquidation value
   b. Real estate investing
   d. Real estate investment trust

18. In economics, business, and accounting, a _____ is the value of money that has been used up to produce something, and hence is not available for use anymore. In business, the _____ may be one of acquisition, in which case the amount of money expended to acquire it is counted as _____. In this case, money is the input that is gone in order to acquire the thing.
   a. Marginal cost
   c. Cost
   b. Sliding scale fees
   d. Fixed costs

19. An _____ is a company whose main business is holding securities of other companies purely for investment purposes. The _____ invests money on behalf of its shareholders who in turn share in the profits and losses.

Chapter 17. Mutual Funds 105

a. AAB
c. Unit investment trust
b. Investment company
d. A Random Walk Down Wall Street

20. A _____ is a periodic payment that is paid by investors in a pooled investment fund to the fund's investment adviser for investment and portfolio management services.

In a mutual fund, the _____ will include any fees payable to the fund's investment adviser or its affiliates, and administrative fees payable to the investment adviser that are not included in the 'Other Expenses' category.)

In a private equity fund, the _____ is an annual payment made by the limited partners in the fund to the fund's manager (e.g., the private equity firm) to pay for the private equity firm's investment operations..

a. 7-Eleven
c. 529 plan
b. 4-4-5 Calendar
d. Management fee

21. The _____ is a financial market where participants buy and sell debt securities, usually in the form of bonds. As of 2006, the size of the international _____ is an estimated $45 trillion, of which the size of the outstanding U.S. _____ debt was $25.2 trillion.

Nearly all of the $923 billion average daily trading volume in the U.S. _____ takes place between broker-dealers and large institutions in a decentralized, over-the-counter market.

a. 4-4-5 Calendar
c. 529 plan
b. Fixed income
d. Bond market

22. A _____ is a listing of bonds or fixed income instruments and a statistic reflecting the composite value of its components. It is used as a tool to represent the characteristics of its component fixed income instruments. They differ from stock market indices in their complexity.
a. Bond market index
c. 7-Eleven
b. 4-4-5 Calendar
d. 529 plan

23. In business and finance, a _____ (also referred to as equity _____) of stock means a _____ of ownership in a corporation (company.) In the plural, stocks is often used as a synonym for _____s especially in the United States, but it is less commonly used that way outside of North America.

In the United Kingdom, South Africa, and Australia, stock can also refer to completely different financial instruments such as government bonds or, less commonly, to all kinds of marketable securities.

a. Bucket shop
c. Procter ' Gamble
b. Margin
d. Share

Chapter 17. Mutual Funds

24. _____ is the trading of a corporation's stock or other securities (e.g. bonds or stock options) by individuals with potential access to non-public information about the company. In most countries, trading by corporate insiders such as officers, key employees, directors, and large shareholders may be legal, if this trading is done in a way that does not take advantage of non-public information. However, the term is frequently used to refer to a practice in which an insider or a related party trades based on material non-public information obtained during the performance of the insider's duties at the corporation, or otherwise in breach of a fiduciary duty or other relationship of trust and confidence or where the non-public information was misappropriated from the company.
   a. Equity investment
   c. Insider Trading
   b. Open outcry
   d. Intellidex

25. In the United States, the Financial Industry Regulatory Authority (FINRA) is a self-regulatory organization (SRO) under the Securities Exchange Act of 1934, successor to the _____.

FINRA is responsible for regulatory oversight of all securities firms that do business with the public; professional training, testing and licensing of registered persons; arbitration and mediation; market regulation by contract for The NASDAQ Stock Market, Inc., the American Stock Exchange LLC, and the International Securities Exchange, LLC; and industry utilities, such as Trade Reporting Facilities and other over-the-counter operations.

   a. 4-4-5 Calendar
   c. 7-Eleven
   b. NASD
   d. 529 plan

26. In the United States, the Financial Industry Regulatory Authority (FINRA) is a self-regulatory organization (SRO) under the Securities Exchange Act of 1934, successor to the _____, Inc.

FINRA is responsible for regulatory oversight of all securities firms that do business with the public; professional training, testing and licensing of registered persons; arbitration and mediation; market regulation by contract for The NASDAQ Stock Market, Inc., the American Stock Exchange LLC, and the International Securities Exchange, LLC; and industry utilities, such as Trade Reporting Facilities and other over-the-counter operations.

   a. National Association of Securities Dealers
   c. 4-4-5 Calendar
   b. 7-Eleven
   d. 529 plan

27. Congress enacted the _____, in the aftermath of the stock market crash of 1929 and during the ensuing Great Depression. It requires that any offer or sale of securities using the means and instrumentalities of interstate commerce be registered pursuant to the 1933 Act, unless an exemption from registration exists under the law.
   a. 7-Eleven
   c. 4-4-5 Calendar
   b. Securities Act of 1933
   d. 529 plan

28. The _____ of 1934 is a law governing the secondary trading of securities (stocks, bonds, and debentures) in the United States of America. The Act, 48 Stat. 881 (enacted June 6, 1934), codified at 15 U.S.C. § 78a et seq., was a sweeping piece of legislation. The Act and related statutes form the basis of regulation of the financial markets and their participants in the United States.
   a. 529 plan
   c. 4-4-5 Calendar
   b. 7-Eleven
   d. Securities Exchange Act

Chapter 17. Mutual Funds

29. _____ is trading executed after the standard local national exchanges have closed. This is distinct from after-hours trading, as they have in context specific meanings, the former may be illegal while the latter is legal.

In the mutual fund context, _____ involves placing orders for mutual fund shares after the close of the stock market, 4:00 p.m for the New York Stock Exchange, but still getting that day's closing price, rather than the next day's opening price.

- a. Certificate in Investment Performance Measurement
- b. Divestment
- c. Tactical asset allocation
- d. Late trading

30. _____ is the strategy of making buy or sell decisions of financial assets (often stocks) by attempting to predict future market price movements. The prediction may be based on an outlook of market or economic conditions resulting from technical or fundamental analysis. This is an investment strategy based on the outlook for an aggregate market, rather than for a particular financial asset.
- a. Portable alpha
- b. Late trading
- c. Market timing
- d. Divestment

Chapter 18. Pension Funds

1. A _____ is a pool of assets forming an independent legal entity that are bought with the contributions to a pension plan for the exclusive purpose of financing pension plan benefits.

   _____s are important shareholders of listed and private companies. They are especially important to the stock market where large institutional investors like the Ontario Teachers' Pension Plan dominate.

   a. Leveraged buyout
   c. Leverage
   b. Limited liability company
   d. Pension fund

2. In financial accounting, the term _____ is most commonly used to describe any part of shareholders' equity, except for basic share capital. Sometimes, the term is used instead of the term provision; such a use, however, is inconsistent with the terminology suggested by International Accounting Standards Board. For more information about provisions, see provision (accounting.)

   a. Treasury stock
   c. Closing entries
   b. FIFO and LIFO accounting
   d. Reserve

3. A _____ is a fungible, negotiable instrument representing financial value. They are broadly categorized into debt securities (such as banknotes, bonds and debentures), and equity securities; e.g., common stocks. The company or other entity issuing the _____ is called the issuer.

   a. Security
   c. Book entry
   b. Tracking stock
   d. Securities lending

4. _____ or financing is to provide capital (funds), which means money for a project, a person, a business or any other private or public institutions.

   Those funds can be allocated for either short term or long term purposes. The health fund is a new way of _____ private healthcare centers.

   a. Proxy fight
   c. Funding
   b. Product life cycle
   d. Synthetic CDO

5. The _____ or forward rate is the agreed upon price of an asset in a forward contract. Using the rational pricing assumption, we can express the _____ in terms of the spot price and any dividends etc., so that there is no possibility for arbitrage.

   The _____ is given by:

Chapter 18. Pension Funds

where

F is the _____ to be paid at time T
e^x is the exponential function
r is the risk-free interest rate
q is the cost-of-carry
S_0 is the spot price of the asset (i.e. what it would sell for at time 0)
D_i is a dividend which is guaranteed to be paid at time t_i where $0 < t_i < T$.

The two questions here are what price the short position (the seller of the asset) should offer to maximize his gain, and what price the long position (the buyer of the asset) should accept to maximize his gain?

At the very least we know that both do not want to lose any money in the deal.

   a. Financial Gerontology   b. Security interest
   c. Biweekly Mortgage   d. Forward price

6.   In finance, a _____ is a forward contract in which one party pays a fixed interest rate, and receives a floating interest rate equal to a reference rate (the underlying rate.) The payments are calculated over a notional amount over a certain period, and netted, i.e. only the differential is paid. It is paid on the effective date.
   a. Triple witching hour   b. Forward rate agreement
   c. PAUG   d. Local volatility

7.   _____ are similar to certificates of deposit that can be purchased at banks; however, they are sold by insurance companies. Like money market funds, they're very safe investments; and like all investments that are considered to be 'very safe', they won't make you very much money. Also known by other names -- fixed-income fund, stable value fund, capital-preservation fund, or guaranteed fund, for example -- they generally pay interest from one- to five years.
   a. Vati-Con   b. CODA plc
   c. Reputational risk   d. Guaranteed investment contracts

8.   A _____ is an exchange of promises between two or more parties to do an act which is enforceable in a court of law. It is where an unqualified offer meets a qualified acceptance and the parties reach Consensus ad Idem. The parties must have the necessary capacity to _____ and the _____ must not be either trifling, indeterminate, impossible or illegal.
   a. 7-Eleven   b. 529 plan
   c. 4-4-5 Calendar   d. Contract

9.   An _____ is a retirement plan account that provides some tax advantages for retirement savings in the United States.
   a. AAB   b. ABN Amro
   c. A Random Walk Down Wall Street   d. Individual Retirement Arrangement

10. _____, in bookkeeping, refers to assets, liabilities, income, and expenses recorded on individual pages of the so called book of final entry or ledger. Changes in _____ value are made by chronologically posting debit (DR) and credit (CR) entries to its page. Examples of _____s are cash, _____s receivable, mortgages, loans, land and buildings, common stock, sales, services provided, wages, and payroll overhead.
   a. Alpha
   b. Option
   c. Accretion
   d. Account

11. The _____ of 1974 (Pub.L. 93-406, 88 Stat. 829, enacted September 2, 1974) is an American federal statute that establishes minimum standards for pension plans in private industry and provides for extensive rules on the federal income tax effects of transactions associated with employee benefit plans.
   a. Express warranty
   b. Articles of Partnership
   c. Expedited Funds Availability Act
   d. Employee Retirement Income Security Act

12. _____, refers to consumption opportunity gained by an entity within a specified time frame, which is generally expressed in monetary terms. However, for households and individuals, '_____ is the sum of all the wages, salaries, profits, interests payments, rents and other forms of earnings received... in a given period of time.' For firms, _____ generally refers to net-profit: what remains of revenue after expenses have been subtracted.
   a. Income
   b. OIBDA
   c. Annual report
   d. Accrual

13. The _____ duty is a legal relationship of confidence or trust between two or more parties, most commonly a _____ or trustee and a principal or beneficiary. One party, for example a corporate trust company or the trust department of a bank, holds a _____ relation or acts in a _____ capacity to another, such as one whose funds are entrusted to it for investment. In a _____ relation one person justifiably reposes confidence, good faith, reliance and trust in another whose aid, advice or protection is sought in some matter.
   a. Financial Institutions Reform Recovery and Enforcement Act
   b. General obligation
   c. Legal tender
   d. Fiduciary

14. The institution most often referenced by the word '_____' is a public or publicly traded _____, the shares of which are traded on a public stock exchange (e.g., the New York Stock Exchange or Nasdaq in the United States) where shares of stock of _____s are bought and sold by and to the general public. Most of the largest businesses in the world are publicly traded _____s. However, the majority of _____s are said to be closely held, privately held or close _____s, meaning that no ready market exists for the trading of shares.
   a. Protect
   b. Federal Home Loan Mortgage Corporation
   c. Depository Trust Company
   d. Corporation

15. _____ is the discipline of identifying, monitoring and limiting risks. In some cases the acceptable risk may be near zero. Risks can come from accidents, natural causes and disasters as well as deliberate attacks from an adversary.
   a. 4-4-5 Calendar
   b. Penny stock
   c. FIFO
   d. Risk management

Chapter 19. Types of Risks Incurred by Financial Institutions

1. _____ is the provision of resources (such as granting a loan) by one party to another party where that second party does not reimburse the first party immediately, thereby generating a debt, and instead arranges either to repay or return those resources (or material(s) of equal value) at a later date. The first party is called a creditor, also known as a lender, while the second party is called a debtor, also known as a borrower.

Movements of financial capital are normally dependent on either _____ or equity transfers.

a. Comparable
b. Warrant
c. Credit
d. Clearing house

2. _____ is the risk of loss due to a debtor's non-payment of a loan or other line of credit (either the principal or interest (coupon) or both)

Most lenders employ their own models (credit scorecards) to rank potential and existing customers according to risk, and then apply appropriate strategies. With products such as unsecured personal loans or mortgages, lenders charge a higher price for higher risk customers and vice versa. With revolving products such as credit cards and overdrafts, risk is controlled through careful setting of credit limits.

a. Market risk
b. Credit risk
c. Liquidity risk
d. Transaction risk

3. _____ is the discipline of identifying, monitoring and limiting risks. In some cases the acceptable risk may be near zero. Risks can come from accidents, natural causes and disasters as well as deliberate attacks from an adversary.

a. 4-4-5 Calendar
b. FIFO
c. Penny stock
d. Risk management

4. _____ is a measure of the ability of a debtor to pay their debts as and when they fall due. It is usually expressed as a ratio or a percentage of current liabilities.

For a corporation with a published balance sheet there are various ratios used to calculate a measure of liquidity.

a. Operating profit margin
b. Operating leverage
c. Invested capital
d. Accounting liquidity

5. _____ arises from situations in which a party interested in trading an asset cannot do it because nobody in the market wants to trade that asset. _____ becomes particularly important to parties who are about to hold or currently hold an asset, since it affects their ability to trade.

Manifestation of _____ is very different from a drop of price to zero.

a. Tracking error
b. Currency risk
c. Credit risk
d. Liquidity risk

6. _____ is a fee paid on borrowed assets. It is the price paid for the use of borrowed money, or, money earned by deposited funds. Assets that are sometimes lent with _____ include money, shares, consumer goods through hire purchase, major assets such as aircraft, and even entire factories in finance lease arrangements.

a. Insolvency
b. Interest
c. AAB
d. A Random Walk Down Wall Street

7. An _____ is the price a borrower pays for the use of money they do not own, and the return a lender receives for deferring the use of funds, by lending it to the borrower. _____s are normally expressed as a percentage rate over the period of one year.

_____s targets are also a vital tool of monetary policy and are used to control variables like investment, inflation, and unemployment.

a. ABN Amro
b. AAB
c. A Random Walk Down Wall Street
d. Interest rate

8. _____ is the risk (variability in value) borne by an interest-bearing asset, such as a loan or a bond, due to variability of interest rates. In general, as rates rise, the price of a fixed rate bond will fall, and vice versa. _____ is commonly measured by the bond's duration.

a. A Random Walk Down Wall Street
b. Official bank rate
c. International Fisher effect
d. Interest rate risk

9. _____ refers to the replacement of an existing debt obligation with a debt obligation bearing different terms. The most common consumer _____ is for a home mortgage.

_____ may be undertaken to reduce interest rate/interest costs (by _____ at a lower rate), to extend the repayment time, to pay off other debt(s), to reduce one's periodic payment obligations (sometimes by taking a longer-term loan), to reduce or alter risk (such as by _____ from a variable-rate to a fixed-rate loan), and/or to raise cash for investment, consumption, or the payment of a dividend.

a. Refinancing
b. 7-Eleven
c. 529 plan
d. 4-4-5 Calendar

10. In banking and finance, _____ is the possibility that a borrower cannot refinance by borrowing to repay existing debt. Many types of commercial lending incorporate bullet payments at the point of final maturity; often, the intention or assumption is that the borrower take out a new loan to pay the existing lenders.

A borrower that cannot refinance its existing debt and does not have sufficient funds on hand to pay its lenders may have a liquidity problem.

a. Refinancing risk
b. Present value
c. Financial transaction
d. Net present value

11. _____ is one of the main genres of financial risk. The term describes the risk that a particular investment might be canceled or stopped somehow, that one may have to find a new place to invest that money with the risk being there might not be a similarly attractive investment available. This primarily occurs if bonds (which are portions of loans to entities) are paid back earlier then expected.

Chapter 19. Types of Risks Incurred by Financial Institutions

a. Biweekly Mortgage
c. Debt cash flow

b. Reinvestment risk
d. Standard of deferred payment

12. _____ is the risk that the value of an investment will decrease due to moves in market factors. The five standard _____ factors are:

- Equity risk, the risk that stock prices will change.
- Interest rate risk, the risk that interest rates will change.
- Currency risk, the risk that foreign exchange rates will change.
- Commodity risk, the risk that commodity prices (e.g. grains, metals) will change.

As with other forms of risk, _____ may be measured in a number of ways. Traditionally, this is done using a Value at Risk methodology. Value at risk is well established as a risk management technique, but it contains a number of limiting assumptions that constrain its accuracy.

a. Transaction risk
c. Currency risk

b. Tracking error
d. Market risk

13. A _____ or bank is a financial institution whose primary activity is to act as a payment agent for customers and to borrow and lend money.

The first modern bank was founded in Italy in Genoa in 1406, its name was Banco di San Giorgio (Bank of St. George.)

Many other financial activities were added over time.

a. Bought deal
c. Black Sea Trade and Development Bank

b. Banker
d. 4-4-5 Calendar

14. In financial mathematics and financial risk management, _____ is a widely used measure of the risk of loss on a specific portfolio of financial assets. For a given portfolio, probability and time horizon, VaR is defined as a threshold value such that the probability that the mark-to-market loss on the portfolio over the given time horizon exceeds this value (assuming normal markets and no trading) is the given probability level.

For example, if a portfolio of stocks has a one-day 5% VaR of $1 million, there is a 5% probability that the portfolio will fall in value by more than $1 million over a one day period, assuming markets are normal and there is no trading.

a. Risk aversion
c. Value at risk

b. Risk modeling
d. Discount factor

15. A standard, commercial _____ is a document issued mostly by a financial institution, used primarily in trade finance, which usually provides an irrevocable payment undertaking.

The _____ can also be the source of payment for a transaction, meaning that redeeming the _____ will pay an exporter. Letters of credit are used primarily in international trade transactions of significant value, for deals between a supplier in one country and a customer in another.

  a. Bond indenture
  b. Duty of loyalty
  c. McFadden Act
  d. Letter of credit

16. _____ is a legally declared inability or impairment of ability of an individual or organization to pay their creditors. Creditors may file a _____ petition against a debtor ('involuntary _____') in an effort to recoup a portion of what they are owed or initiate a restructuring. In the majority of cases, however, _____ is initiated by the debtor (a 'voluntary _____' that is filed by the bankrupt individual or organization.)

  a. 4-4-5 Calendar
  b. Debt settlement
  c. 529 plan
  d. Bankruptcy

17. When companies conduct business across borders, they must deal in foreign currencies. Companies must exchange foreign currencies for home currencies when dealing with receivables, and vice versa for payables. This is done at the current exchange rate between the two countries. _____ is the risk that the exchange rate will change unfavorably before the currency is exchanged.

  a. 529 plan
  b. Foreign exchange risk
  c. Lower of cost or market rule
  d. 4-4-5 Calendar

18. The _____ was a period of financial crisis that gripped much of Asia beginning in July 1997, and raised fears of a worldwide economic meltdown (financial contagion).

The crisis started in Thailand with the financial collapse of the Thai baht caused by the decision of the Thai government to float the baht, cutting its peg to the USD, after exhaustive efforts to support it in the face of a severe financial overextension that was in part real estate driven. At the time, Thailand had acquired a burden of foreign debt that made the country effectively bankrupt even before the collapse of its currency.

  a. Asian Financial Crisis
  b. OTC Bulletin Board
  c. International trade
  d. Internal control

19. _____ refers to the likelihood that changes in the business environment adversely affect operating profits or the value of assets in a specific country. For example, financial factors such as currency controls, devaluation or regulatory changes, or stability factors such as mass riots, civil war and other potential events contribute to companies' operational risks. This term is also sometimes referred to as political risk, however _____ is a more general term, which generally only refers to risks affecting all companies operating within a particular country.

  a. Country risk
  b. Single-index model
  c. Capital asset
  d. Solvency

20. An _____ is a risk arising from execution of a company's business functions. As such, it is a very broad concept including e.g. fraud risks, legal risks, physical or environmental risks, etc. The term _____ is most commonly found in risk management programs of financial institutions that must organize their risk management program according to Basel II.

Chapter 19. Types of Risks Incurred by Financial Institutions 115

    a. AAB
    b. A Random Walk Down Wall Street
    c. ABN Amro
    d. Operational risk

21. _____ and the related Fisher's linear discriminant are methods used in statistics and machine learning to find the linear combination of features which best separate two or more classes of objects or events. The resulting combination may be used as a linear classifier, or, more commonly, for dimensionality reduction before later classification.

_____ is closely related to ANOVA (analysis of variance) and regression analysis, which also attempt to express one dependent variable as a linear combination of other features or measurements.

    a. 4-4-5 Calendar
    b. Linear discriminant analysis
    c. 529 plan
    d. 7-Eleven

22. A _____ is a fungible, negotiable instrument representing financial value. They are broadly categorized into debt securities (such as banknotes, bonds and debentures), and equity securities; e.g., common stocks. The company or other entity issuing the _____ is called the issuer.
    a. Securities lending
    b. Tracking stock
    c. Book entry
    d. Security

23. _____ means the inability to pay one's debts as they fall due. Usually used in Business terms, _____ refers to the inability for a 'limited liability' company to pay off debts.

This is defined in two different ways:

Cash flow _____ -
    Unable to pay debts as they fall due.
Balance sheet _____ -
    Having negative net assets: liabilities exceed assets; or net liabilities.

    a. Interest
    b. Insolvency
    c. AAB
    d. A Random Walk Down Wall Street

24. In finance, the _____ of a financial asset measures the sensitivity of the asset's price to interest rate movements, expressed as a number of years. The reason for expressing this sensitivity in years is that the time that will elapse until a cash flow is received allows more interest to accumulate. Therefore the price of an asset with long term cashflows has more interest rate sensitivity than an asset with cashflows in the near future.
    a. 4-4-5 Calendar
    b. Yield to maturity
    c. Macaulay duration
    d. Duration

25. In economics, _____ is a rise in the general level of prices of goods and services in an economy over a period of time. The term '_____' once referred to increases in the money supply (monetary _____); however, economic debates about the relationship between money supply and price levels have led to its primary use today in describing price _____.
_____ can also be described as a decline in the real value of money--a loss of purchasing power in the medium of exchange which is also the monetary unit of account.

a. ABN Amro
b. AAB
c. A Random Walk Down Wall Street
d. Inflation

26. _____ is a branch of economics that deals with the performance, structure, and behavior of a national or regional economy as a whole. Along with microeconomics, _____ is one of the two most general fields in economics. Macroeconomists study aggregated indicators such as GDP, unemployment rates, and price indices to understand how the whole economy functions.

a. Macroeconomics
b. Recession
c. Behavioral finance
d. Human capital

Chapter 20. Managing Credit Risk on the Balance Sheet

1. In financial accounting, a _____ or statement of financial position is a summary of a person's or organization's balances. Assets, liabilities and ownership equity are listed as of a specific date, such as the end of its financial year. A _____ is often described as a snapshot of a company's financial condition.
   a. Financial statements
   b. Statement of retained earnings
   c. Statement on Auditing Standards No. 70: Service Organizations
   d. Balance sheet

2. _____ is the provision of resources (such as granting a loan) by one party to another party where that second party does not reimburse the first party immediately, thereby generating a debt, and instead arranges either to repay or return those resources (or material(s) of equal value) at a later date. The first party is called a creditor, also known as a lender, while the second party is called a debtor, also known as a borrower.

    Movements of financial capital are normally dependent on either _____ or equity transfers.

   a. Credit
   b. Warrant
   c. Comparable
   d. Clearing house

3. _____ is the risk of loss due to a debtor's non-payment of a loan or other line of credit (either the principal or interest (coupon) or both)

    Most lenders employ their own models (credit scorecards) to rank potential and existing customers according to risk, and then apply appropriate strategies. With products such as unsecured personal loans or mortgages, lenders charge a higher price for higher risk customers and vice versa. With revolving products such as credit cards and overdrafts, risk is controlled through careful setting of credit limits.

   a. Liquidity risk
   b. Market risk
   c. Transaction risk
   d. Credit risk

4. _____ is the method by which one calculates the creditworthiness of a business or organization. The audited financial statements of a large company might be analyzed when it issues or has issued bonds. Or, a bank may analyze the financial statements of a small business before making or renewing a commercial loan.
   a. Credit report monitoring
   b. Credit crunch
   c. Credit analysis
   d. Capital note

5. Risk adjusted return on capital (_____) is a risk-based profitability measurement framework for analysing risk-adjusted financial performance and providing a consistent view of profitability across businesses. The concept was developed by Bankers Trust in the late 1970s. Note, however, that more and more Risk Adjusted Return on Risk Adjusted Capital (RARORAC) is used as a measure, whereby the risk adjustment of Capital is based on the capital adequacy guidelines as outlined by the Basel Committee, currently Basel II.
   a. Risk modeling
   b. Value at risk
   c. Discount factor
   d. RAROC

6. In statistics, a _____ is a dimensionless quantity derived by subtracting the population mean from an individual raw score and then dividing the difference by the population standard deviation. This conversion process is called standardizing or normalizing; however, 'normalizing' can refer to many types of ratios; see normalization (statistics) for more.

_____s are also called z-values, z-scores, normal scores, and standardized variables; the use of 'Z' is because the normal distribution is also known as the 'Z distribution'.

- a. Monte Carlo methods
- b. Semivariance
- c. Normal distribution
- d. Standard score

7. _____ is that which is owed; usually referencing assets owed, but the term can cover other obligations. In the case of assets, _____ is a means of using future purchasing power in the present before a summation has been earned. Some companies and corporations use _____ as a part of their overall corporate finance strategy.
- a. Credit cycle
- b. Partial Payment
- c. Cross-collateralization
- d. Debt

8. _____ is the legal and professional proceeding in which a mortgagee usually a lender, obtains a court ordered termination of a mortgagor's equitable right of redemption. Usually a lender obtains a security interest from a borrower who mortgages or pledges an asset like a house to secure the loan. If the borrower defaults and the lender tries to repossess the property, courts of equity can grant the borrower the equitable right of redemption if the borrower repays the debt.
- a. Liability
- b. Letter of credit
- c. Federal Acquisition Regulations
- d. Foreclosure

9. In lending agreements, _____ is a borrower's pledge of specific property to a lender, to secure repayment of a loan. The _____ serves as protection for a lender against a borrower's risk of default - that is, a borrower failing to pay the principal and interest under the terms of a loan obligation. If a borrower does default on a loan (due to insolvency or other event), that borrower forfeits (gives up) the property pledged as _____ *ollateral* - and the lender then becomes the owner of the _____.
- a. Future-oriented
- b. Nominal value
- c. Refinancing risk
- d. Collateral

10. A _____ is a party (e.g. person, organization, company, or government) that has a claim to the services of a second party. The first party, in general, has provided some property or service to the second party under the assumption (usually enforced by contract) that the second party will return an equivalent property or service. The second party is frequently called a debtor or borrower.
- a. Redemption value
- b. False billing
- c. NOPLAT
- d. Creditor

11. The _____ of an asset is the return obtained from holding it (if positive), or the cost of holding it (if negative)

For instance, commodities are usually negative _____ assets, as they incur storage costs, but in some circumstances, commodities can be positive _____ assets as the market is willing to pay a premium for availability.

This can also refer to a trade with more than one leg, where you earn the spread between borrowing a low _____ asset and lending a high _____ one.

Chapter 20. Managing Credit Risk on the Balance Sheet

a. Cramdown
b. Bankruptcy remote
c. Carry
d. Financial assistance

12. _____ is the balance of the amounts of cash being received and paid by a business during a defined period of time, sometimes tied to a specific project. Measurement of _____ can be used

- to evaluate the state or performance of a business or project.
- to determine problems with liquidity. Being profitable does not necessarily mean being liquid. A company can fail because of a shortage of cash, even while profitable.
- to generate project rate of returns. The time of _____s into and out of projects are used as inputs to financial models such as internal rate of return, and net present value.
- to examine income or growth of a business when it is believed that accrual accounting concepts do not represent economic realities. Alternately, _____ can be used to 'validate' the net income generated by accrual accounting.

_____ as a generic term may be used differently depending on context, and certain _____ definitions may be adapted by analysts and users for their own uses. Common terms include operating _____ and free _____.

_____s can be classified into:

1. Operational _____s: Cash received or expended as a result of the company's core business activities.
2. Investment _____s: Cash received or expended through capital expenditure, investments or acquisitions.
3. Financing _____s: Cash received or expended as a result of financial activities, such as interests and dividends.

All three together - the net _____ - are necessary to reconcile the beginning cash balance to the ending cash balance. Loan draw downs or equity injections, that is just shifting of capital but no expenditure as such, are not considered in the net _____.

a. Corporate finance
b. Cash flow
c. Shareholder value
d. Real option

13. In financial accounting, a _____ or statement of cash flows is a financial statement that shows a company's flow of cash. The money coming into the business is called cash inflow, and money going out from the business is called cash outflow. The statement shows how changes in balance sheet and income accounts affect cash and cash equivalents, and breaks the analysis down to operating, investing, and financing activities.

a. 529 plan
b. Cash flow statement
c. 7-Eleven
d. 4-4-5 Calendar

14. In finance, a _____ or accounting ratio is a ratio of two selected numerical values taken from an enterprise's financial statements. There are many standard ratios used to try to evaluate the overall financial condition of a corporation or other organization. They may be used by managers within a firm, by current and potential shareholders (owners) of a firm, and by a firm's creditors. Security analysts use these to compare the strengths and weaknesses in various companies.

a. Sustainable growth rate
b. Price/cash flow ratio
c. Return on capital employed
d. Financial ratio

15. _____ or financing is to provide capital (funds), which means money for a project, a person, a business or any other private or public institutions.

Those funds can be allocated for either short term or long term purposes. The health fund is a new way of _____ private healthcare centers.

a. Proxy fight
b. Synthetic CDO
c. Product life cycle
d. Funding

16. In finance, the Acid-test or _____ or liquid ratio measures the ability of a company to use its near cash or quick assets to immediately extinguish or retire its current liabilities. Quick assets include those current assets that presumably can be quickly converted to cash at close to their book values.

Generally, the acid test ratio should be 1:1 or better, however this varies widely by industry.

a. Quick ratio
b. Financial ratio
c. P/E ratio
d. Net assets

17. The _____ is a financial ratio that measures whether or not a firm has enough resources to pay its debts over the next 12 months. It compares a firm's current assets to its current liabilities. It is expressed as follows:

$$\text{Current ratio} = \frac{\text{Current Assets}}{\text{Current Liabilities}}$$

For example, if WXY Company's current assets are $50,000,000 and its current liabilities are $40,000,000, then its _____ would be $50,000,000 divided by $40,000,000, which equals 1.25.

a. PEG ratio
b. Sustainable growth rate
c. Debt service coverage ratio
d. Current ratio

18. _____ is a measure of the ability of a debtor to pay their debts as and when they fall due. It is usually expressed as a ratio or a percentage of current liabilities.

For a corporation with a published balance sheet there are various ratios used to calculate a measure of liquidity.

a. Invested capital
b. Operating profit margin
c. Operating leverage
d. Accounting liquidity

19. In business and accounting, _____s are everything of value that is owned by a person or company. The balance sheet of a firm records the monetary value of the _____s owned by the firm. The two major _____ classes are tangible _____s and intangible _____s.

a. Accounts payable
b. Asset
c. Income
d. EBITDA

20. The term _____ is often used to refer to the investment management of collective investments, (not necessarily) whilst the more generic fund management may refer to all forms of institutional investment as well as investment management for private investors. Investment managers who specialize in advisory or discretionary management on behalf of (normally wealthy) private investors may often refer to their services as wealth management or portfolio management often within the context of so-called 'private banking'.

The provision of 'investment management services' includes elements of financial analysis, asset selection, stock selection, plan implementation and ongoing monitoring of investments.

a. A Random Walk Down Wall Street
b. ABN Amro
c. Asset management
d. AAB

21. _____ is a business term and may be used as a broad measure of asset efficiency and is calculated by dividing sales revenue by the total assets.

It's also used in the Du Pont Identity:

$$\frac{Net\ Earnings}{Shareholders\ Eq.} = \frac{Net\ Earnings}{Sales(Income)} * \frac{Sales(Income)}{Total Assets} * \frac{Total\ Assets}{Shareholders\ Eq.}$$

In which,

$$Net\ Margin = \frac{Net\ Earnings}{Sales(Income)}$$
$$Total\ Asset\ Turnover = \frac{Sales(Income)}{Total Assets}$$
$$Financial\ Leverage = \frac{Average\ Total\ Assets}{Average\ Total\ Equity}$$

The net margin is a summary indicator of an income statement, Asset turnover is an indicator of the left side of the balance sheet (total assets' side) and Leverage is an indicator of the right side of the Balance Sheet (liabilities and shareholders' equity' side.)

The Du Pont Identity helps many companies or individuals, visualize and comprehend the analysis of a financial statement or annual report of a company, in return on assets and return on investments.

a. Operating profit margin
b. Earnings yield
c. Invested capital
d. Assets turnover

Chapter 20. Managing Credit Risk on the Balance Sheet

22. _____ plant, and equipment, is a term used in accountancy for assets and property which cannot easily be converted into cash. This can be compared with current assets such as cash or bank accounts, which are described as liquid assets. In most cases, only tangible assets are referred to as fixed.
   a. Remittance advice
   b. Petty cash
   c. Percentage of Completion
   d. Fixed asset

23. _____ is a list for goods and materials held available in stock by a business. It is also used for a list of the contents of a household and for a list for testamentary purposes of the possessions of someone who has died. In accounting _____ is considered an asset.
   a. A Random Walk Down Wall Street
   b. Inventory
   c. ABN Amro
   d. AAB

24. _____ is a financial metric which represents operating liquidity available to a business. Along with fixed assets such as plant and equipment, _____ is considered a part of operating capital. It is calculated as current assets minus current liabilities.
   a. Working capital management
   b. 529 plan
   c. Working capital
   d. 4-4-5 Calendar

25. In financial and business accounting, _____ is a measure of a firm's profitability that excludes interest and income tax expenses.

EBIT = Operating Revenue - Operating Expenses (OPEX) + Non-operating Income

Operating Income = Operating Revenue - Operating Expenses

Operating income is the difference between operating revenues and operating expenses, but it is also sometimes used as a synonym for EBIT and operating profit. This is true if the firm has no non-operating income.

   a. A Random Walk Down Wall Street
   b. ABN Amro
   c. AAB
   d. Earnings before interest and taxes

26. _____ is the value on a given date of a future payment or series of future payments, discounted to reflect the time value of money and other factors such as investment risk. _____ calculations are widely used in business and economics to provide a means to compare cash flows at different times on a meaningful 'like to like' basis.

The most commonly applied model of the time value of money is compound interest.

   a. Present value of benefits
   b. Net present value
   c. Negative gearing
   d. Present value

27. _____ is a fee paid on borrowed assets. It is the price paid for the use of borrowed money, or, money earned by deposited funds. Assets that are sometimes lent with _____ include money, shares, consumer goods through hire purchase, major assets such as aircraft, and even entire factories in finance lease arrangements.
   a. AAB
   b. Insolvency
   c. A Random Walk Down Wall Street
   d. Interest

Chapter 20. Managing Credit Risk on the Balance Sheet

28. In finance, _____ is the ability of an entity to pay its debts with available cash. _____ can also be described as the ability of a corporation to meet its long-term fixed expenses and to accomplish long-term expansion and growth. The better a company's _____, the better it is financially.
   a. Capital asset
   c. Political risk
   b. Mid price
   d. Solvency

29. A _____ is a payment made by a corporation to its shareholder members. When a corporation earns a profit or surplus, that money can be put to two uses: it can either be re-invested in the business (called retained earnings), or it can be paid to the shareholders as a _____. Many corporations retain a portion of their earnings and pay the remainder as a _____.
   a. Dividend
   c. Dividend yield
   b. Special dividend
   d. Dividend puzzle

30. _____, Gross profit margin or Gross Profit Rate can be defined as the amount of contribution to the business enterprise, after paying for direct-fixed and direct-variable unit costs, required to cover overheads (fixed commitments) and provide a buffer for unknown items. It expresses the relationship between gross profit and sales revenue.

It can be expressed in absolute terms:

Gross Profit = Revenue >− Cost of Goods Sold

or as the ratio of gross profit to sales revenue, usually in the form of a percentage:

_____ Percentage = (Revenue-Cost of Goods Sold)/Revenue

Cost of goods sold includes variable costs and fixed costs directly linked to the product, such as material and labor. It does not include indirect fixed costs like office expenses, rent, administrative costs, etc.

   a. Profit margin
   c. Net profit margin
   b. 4-4-5 Calendar
   d. Gross margin

31. _____ is a measure of a company's earning power from ongoing operations, equal to earnings before the deduction of interest payments and income taxes.

To accountants, economic profit, or EP, is a single-period metric to determine the value created by a company in one period - usually a year. It is the net profit after tax less the equity charge, a risk-weighted cost of capital.

   a. A Random Walk Down Wall Street
   c. Operating profit
   b. Economic profit
   d. AAB

32. In business, operating margin, operating income margin, _____ or return on sales (ROS) is the ratio of operating income (operating profit in the UK) divided by net sales, usually presented in percent.

(Relevant figures in italics)

It is a measurement of what proportion of a company's revenue is left over, before taxes and other indirect costs (such as rent, bonus, interest, etc.), after paying for variable costs of production as wages, raw materials, etc. A good operating margin is needed for a company to be able to pay for its fixed costs, such as interest on debt.

   a. Interest coverage ratio   b. Operating leverage
   c. Average rate of return   d. Operating profit margin

33. _____ measures the rate of return on the ownership interest (shareholders' equity) of the common stock owners. _____ is viewed as one of the most important financial ratios. It measures a firm's efficiency at generating profits from every dollar of shareholders' equity (also known as net assets or assets minus liabilities.)
   a. Return on sales   b. Return of capital
   c. Diluted Earnings Per Share   d. Return on equity

34. The _____ percentage shows how profitable a company's assets are in generating revenue.

_____ can be computed as:

$$ROA = \frac{\text{Net Income}}{\text{Total Assets}}$$

This number tells you 'what the company can do with what it's got', i.e. how many dollars of earnings they derive from each dollar of assets they control. It's a useful number for comparing competing companies in the same industry.

   a. Return on sales   b. Receivables turnover ratio
   c. P/E ratio   d. Return on assets

35. In economics, business, and accounting, a _____ is the value of money that has been used up to produce something, and hence is not available for use anymore. In business, the _____ may be one of acquisition, in which case the amount of money expended to acquire it is counted as _____. In this case, money is the input that is gone in order to acquire the thing.
   a. Marginal cost   b. Fixed costs
   c. Cost   d. Sliding scale fees

36. In finance, a _____ is collateral that the holder of a position in securities, options, or futures contracts has to deposit to cover the credit risk of his counterparty (most often his broker.) This risk can arise if the holder has done any of the following:

- borrowed cash from the counterparty to buy securities or options,
- sold securities or options short, or
- entered into a futures contract.

The collateral can be in the form of cash or securities, and it is deposited in a _____ account. On U.S. futures exchanges, '_____' was formally called performance bond.

_____ buying is buying securities with cash borrowed from a broker, using other securities as collateral.

a. Credit
b. Margin
c. Procter ' Gamble
d. Share

37. _____ is the price at which an asset would trade in a competitive Walrasian auction setting. _____ is often used interchangeably with open _____, fair value or fair _____, although these terms have distinct definitions in different standards, and may differ in some circumstances.

International Valuation Standards defines _____ as 'the estimated amount for which a property should exchange on the date of valuation between a willing buyer and a willing seller in an arm'e;s-length transaction after proper marketing wherein the parties had each acted knowledgeably, prudently, and without compulsion.'

_____ is a concept distinct from market price, which is 'e;the price at which one can transact'e;, while _____ is 'e;the true underlying value'e; according to theoretical standards.

a. Wrap account
b. T-Model
c. Debt restructuring
d. Market value

38. _____ is the difference between price and the costs of bringing to market whatever it is that is accounted as an enterprise (whether by harvest, extraction, manufacture, or purchase) in terms of the component costs of delivered goods and/or services and any operating or other expenses.

A key difficulty in measuring profit is in defining costs. Pure economic monetary profits can be zero or negative even in competitive equilibrium when accounted monetized costs exceed monetized price.

a. Economic profit
b. A Random Walk Down Wall Street
c. AAB
d. Accounting profit

39. _____, Net Margin, Net _____ or Net Profit Ratio all refer to a measure of profitability. It is calculated using a formula and written as a percentage or a number.

$$\text{Net profit margin} = \frac{\text{Net profit after taxes}}{\text{Net Sales}}$$

The _____ is mostly used for internal comparison.

a. Profit margin
c. Net profit margin
b. 4-4-5 Calendar
d. Profit maximization

40. The institution most often referenced by the word '_____' is a public or publicly traded _____, the shares of which are traded on a public stock exchange (e.g., the New York Stock Exchange or Nasdaq in the United States) where shares of stock of _____s are bought and sold by and to the general public. Most of the largest businesses in the world are publicly traded _____s. However, the majority of _____s are said to be closely held, privately held or close _____s, meaning that no ready market exists for the trading of shares.

a. Federal Home Loan Mortgage Corporation
c. Protect
b. Depository Trust Company
d. Corporation

41. In finance, _____ occurs when a debtor has not met its legal obligations according to the debt contract, e.g. it has not made a scheduled payment, or has violated a loan covenant (condition) of the debt contract. _____ may occur if the debtor is either unwilling or unable to pay their debt. This can occur with all debt obligations including bonds, mortgages, loans, and promissory notes.

a. Vendor finance
c. Debt validation
b. Credit crunch
d. Default

42. The _____ (LIBID) is a bid rate; the rate bid by banks on Eurocurrency deposits (i.e., the rate at which a bank is willing to borrow from other banks.) It is 'the opposite' of the LIBOR (an offered, hence 'ask' rate.) Whilst the British Bankers' Association set LIBOR rates, there is no correspondent official LIBID fixing.

a. Repo rate
c. Shanghai Interbank Offered Rate
b. Cash accumulation equation
d. London Interbank Bid Rate

43. The _____ is a daily reference rate based on the interest rates at which banks borrow unsecured funds from banks in the London wholesale money market (or interbank market.) It is roughly comparable to the U.S. Federal funds rate.

During 1984 it became apparent that an increasing number of banks were trading actively in a variety of relatively new market instruments, notably interest rate swaps, foreign currency options and forward rate agreements.

a. Shanghai Interbank Offered Rate
c. Risk-free interest rate
b. Fixed interest
d. London Interbank Offered Rate

44. _____ is a term applied in many countries to a reference interest rate used by banks. The term originally indicated the rate of interest at which banks lent to favored customers, i.e., those with high credibility, though this is no longer always the case. Some variable interest rates may be expressed as a percentage above or below _____.

a. Reserve requirement
c. Credit bureau
b. Prime rate
d. Time deposit

45. In financial accounting, the term _____ is most commonly used to describe any part of shareholders' equity, except for basic share capital. Sometimes, the term is used instead of the term provision; such a use, however, is inconsistent with the terminology suggested by International Accounting Standards Board. For more information about provisions, see provision (accounting.)

Chapter 20. Managing Credit Risk on the Balance Sheet

a. FIFO and LIFO accounting
c. Treasury stock
b. Closing entries
d. Reserve

46. The _____ is a bank regulation that sets the minimum reserves each bank must hold to customer deposits and notes. These reserves are designed to satisfy withdrawal demands, and would normally be in the form of fiat currency stored in a bank vault (vault cash), or with a central bank.

The reserve ratio is sometimes used as a tool in the monetary policy, influencing the country's economy, borrowing, and interest rates.

a. Variable rate mortgage
c. Wall Street Journal prime rate
b. Reserve requirement
d. Prime rate

47. A _____ or bank is a financial institution whose primary activity is to act as a payment agent for customers and to borrow and lend money.

The first modern bank was founded in Italy in Genoa in 1406, its name was Banco di San Giorgio (Bank of St. George.)

Many other financial activities were added over time.

a. Banker
c. Bought deal
b. 4-4-5 Calendar
d. Black Sea Trade and Development Bank

48. _____ arises from situations in which a party interested in trading an asset cannot do it because nobody in the market wants to trade that asset. _____ becomes particularly important to parties who are about to hold or currently hold an asset, since it affects their ability to trade.

Manifestation of _____ is very different from a drop of price to zero.

a. Currency risk
c. Credit risk
b. Liquidity risk
d. Tracking error

Chapter 21. Managing Liquidity Risk on the Balance Sheet

1. _____ is a fee paid on borrowed assets. It is the price paid for the use of borrowed money, or, money earned by deposited funds. Assets that are sometimes lent with _____ include money, shares, consumer goods through hire purchase, major assets such as aircraft, and even entire factories in finance lease arrangements.
   a. Insolvency
   b. AAB
   c. A Random Walk Down Wall Street
   d. Interest

2. An _____ is the price a borrower pays for the use of money they do not own, and the return a lender receives for deferring the use of funds, by lending it to the borrower. _____s are normally expressed as a percentage rate over the period of one year.

   _____s targets are also a vital tool of monetary policy and are used to control variables like investment, inflation, and unemployment.

   a. ABN Amro
   b. A Random Walk Down Wall Street
   c. Interest rate
   d. AAB

3. _____ is a measure of the ability of a debtor to pay their debts as and when they fall due. It is usually expressed as a ratio or a percentage of current liabilities.

   For a corporation with a published balance sheet there are various ratios used to calculate a measure of liquidity.

   a. Operating leverage
   b. Invested capital
   c. Operating profit margin
   d. Accounting liquidity

4. _____ arises from situations in which a party interested in trading an asset cannot do it because nobody in the market wants to trade that asset. _____ becomes particularly important to parties who are about to hold or currently hold an asset, since it affects their ability to trade.

   Manifestation of _____ is very different from a drop of price to zero.

   a. Liquidity risk
   b. Currency risk
   c. Credit risk
   d. Tracking error

5. In financial accounting, a _____ or statement of financial position is a summary of a person's or organization's balances. Assets, liabilities and ownership equity are listed as of a specific date, such as the end of its financial year. A _____ is often described as a snapshot of a company's financial condition.
   a. Financial statements
   b. Balance sheet
   c. Statement of retained earnings
   d. Statement on Auditing Standards No. 70: Service Organizations

6. In the most general sense, a _____ is anything that is a hindrance, or puts individuals at a disadvantage.

   Before we discuss the financial terms, we should note that a _____ can also have a much more important slang meaning.

   This is best described in an example.

Chapter 21. Managing Liquidity Risk on the Balance Sheet

a. Limited liability
b. McFadden Act
c. Covenant
d. Liability

7. _____ is a life of security. It may also refer to the final payment date of a loan or other financial instrument, at which point all remaining interest and principal is due to be paid.

1, 3, 6 months _____ band can be calculated by using 30-day per month periods.

a. Replacement cost
b. False billing
c. Primary market
d. Maturity

8. In business and accounting, _____s are everything of value that is owned by a person or company. The balance sheet of a firm records the monetary value of the _____s owned by the firm. The two major _____ classes are tangible _____s and intangible _____s.

a. Income
b. EBITDA
c. Accounts payable
d. Asset

9. _____ is a structured finance process that involves pooling and repackaging of cash-flow-producing financial assets into securities, which are then sold to investors. The term '_____' is derived from the fact that the form of financial instruments used to obtain funds from the investors are securities. As a portfolio risk backed by amortizing cash flows - and unlike general corporate debt - the credit quality of securitized debt is non-stationary due to changes in volatility that are time- and structure-dependent.

a. The Glass-Steagall Act of 1933
b. Securitization
c. Reputational risk
d. Special journals

10. _____ or financing is to provide capital (funds), which means money for a project, a person, a business or any other private or public institutions.

Those funds can be allocated for either short term or long term purposes. The health fund is a new way of _____ private healthcare centers.

a. Funding
b. Proxy fight
c. Synthetic CDO
d. Product life cycle

11. _____ is a process of analyzing possible future events by considering alternative possible outcomes (scenarios.) The analysis is designed to allow improved decision-making by allowing consideration of outcomes and their implications.

For example, in economics and finance, a financial institution might attempt to forecast several possible scenarios for the economy (e.g. rapid growth, moderate growth, slow growth) and it might also attempt to forecast financial market returns (for bonds, stocks and cash) in each of those scenarios.

a. 4-4-5 Calendar
b. Detection Risk
c. 529 plan
d. Scenario analysis

Chapter 21. Managing Liquidity Risk on the Balance Sheet

12. A _____ is a financial crisis that occurs when many banks suffer runs at the same time. A systemic banking crisis is one where all or almost all of the banking capital in a country is wiped out. The resulting chain of bankruptcies can cause a long economic recession. Much of the Great Depression's economic damage was caused directly by bank runs. The cost of cleaning up a systemic banking crisis can be huge, with fiscal costs averaging 13% of GDP and economic output losses averaging 20% of GDP for important crises from 1970 to 2007.
    a. Banking panic
    b. Credit bureau
    c. Deposit insurance
    d. Probability of default

13. _____ is a type of bank account where the money in the account is legally able to be withdrawn immediately upon demand (or 'at call'.) This type of bank account can also be referred to as a 'cheque' or 'checking' or transactional account.

    This type of bank account, allowing immediate conversion of the account balance into cash or withdrawal to another account, can be contrasted with a time deposit (also known as a certificate of deposit or term deposit), where the funds are not legally available for immediate withdrawal by the depositor.

    a. 4-4-5 Calendar
    b. 529 plan
    c. Synthetic lease
    d. Demand deposit

14. Explicit _____ is a measure implemented in many countries to protect bank depositors, in full or in part, from losses caused by a bank's inability to pay its debts when due. _____ systems are one component of a financial system safety net that promotes financial stability.
    a. Reserve requirement
    b. Time deposit
    c. Deposit insurance
    d. Banking panic

15. A '_____' is a 'Charge' that is paid to obtain the right to delay a payment. Essentially, the payer purchases the right to make a given payment in the future instead of in the Present. The '_____', or 'Charge' that must be paid to delay the payment, is simply the difference between what the payment amount would be if it were paid in the present and what the payment amount would be paid if it were paid in the future.
    a. Risk modeling
    b. Value at risk
    c. Risk aversion
    d. Discount

16. The _____ is an interest rate a central bank charges depository institutions that borrow reserves from it.

    The term _____ has two meanings:

    - the same as interest rate; the term 'discount' does not refer to the meaning of the word, but to the purpose of using the quantity, such as computations of present value, e.g. net present value / discounted cash flow

    - the annual effective _____, which is the annual interest divided by the capital including that interest; this rate is lower than the interest rate; it corresponds to using the value after a year as the nominal value, and seeing the initial value as the nominal value minus a discount; it is used for Treasury Bills and similar financial instruments

    The annual effective _____ is the annual interest divided by the capital including that interest, which is the interest rate divided by 100% plus the interest rate. It is the annual discount factor to be applied to the future cash flow, to find the discount, subtracted from a future value to find the value one year earlier.

For example, suppose there is a government bond that sells for $95 and pays $100 in a year's time.

   a. Black-Scholes
   b. Stochastic volatility
   c. Fisher equation
   d. Discount rate

17. _____ is a stock market index for the Tokyo Stock Exchange (TSE.) It has been calculated daily by the Nihon Keizai Shimbun (Nikkei) newspaper since 1950. It is a price-weighted average (the unit is Yen), and the components are reviewed once a year.

   a. 4-4-5 Calendar
   b. 529 plan
   c. 7-Eleven
   d. Nikkei 225

18. _____ is the provision of resources (such as granting a loan) by one party to another party where that second party does not reimburse the first party immediately, thereby generating a debt, and instead arranges either to repay or return those resources (or material(s) of equal value) at a later date. The first party is called a creditor, also known as a lender, while the second party is called a debtor, also known as a borrower.

Movements of financial capital are normally dependent on either _____ or equity transfers.

   a. Clearing house
   b. Credit
   c. Comparable
   d. Warrant

19. A _____ is a professionally managed type of collective investment scheme that pools money from many investors and invests it in stocks, bonds, short-term money market instruments, and/or other securities. The _____ will have a fund manager that trades the pooled money on a regular basis. Currently, the worldwide value of all _____s totals more than $26 trillion.

Since 1940, there have been three basic types of investment companies in the United States: open-end funds, also known in the US as _____s; unit investment trusts (UITs); and closed-end funds.

   a. Trust company
   b. Financial intermediary
   c. Net asset value
   d. Mutual fund

Chapter 22. Managing Interest Rate Risk and Insolvency Risk on the Balance Sheet

1. _____ is a fee paid on borrowed assets. It is the price paid for the use of borrowed money, or, money earned by deposited funds. Assets that are sometimes lent with _____ include money, shares, consumer goods through hire purchase, major assets such as aircraft, and even entire factories in finance lease arrangements.
   a. Insolvency
   b. A Random Walk Down Wall Street
   c. AAB
   d. Interest

2. An _____ is the price a borrower pays for the use of money they do not own, and the return a lender receives for deferring the use of funds, by lending it to the borrower. _____s are normally expressed as a percentage rate over the period of one year.

   _____s targets are also a vital tool of monetary policy and are used to control variables like investment, inflation, and unemployment.
   a. ABN Amro
   b. AAB
   c. A Random Walk Down Wall Street
   d. Interest rate

3. _____ is the discipline of identifying, monitoring and limiting risks. In some cases the acceptable risk may be near zero. Risks can come from accidents, natural causes and disasters as well as deliberate attacks from an adversary.
   a. Risk management
   b. Penny stock
   c. 4-4-5 Calendar
   d. FIFO

4. A _____ is a financial contract whose value is derived from the value of something else (known as the underlying.) The underlying on which a _____ is based can be an asset, weather conditions bonds or other forms of credit.
   a. 4-4-5 Calendar
   b. 7-Eleven
   c. 529 plan
   d. Derivative

5. _____ is the risk (variability in value) borne by an interest-bearing asset, such as a loan or a bond, due to variability of interest rates. In general, as rates rise, the price of a fixed rate bond will fall, and vice versa. _____ is commonly measured by the bond's duration.
   a. Official bank rate
   b. International Fisher effect
   c. A Random Walk Down Wall Street
   d. Interest rate risk

6. _____ or financing is to provide capital (funds), which means money for a project, a person, a business or any other private or public institutions.

   Those funds can be allocated for either short term or long term purposes. The health fund is a new way of _____ private healthcare centers.
   a. Funding
   b. Proxy fight
   c. Product life cycle
   d. Synthetic CDO

7. In business and accounting, _____s are everything of value that is owned by a person or company. The balance sheet of a firm records the monetary value of the _____s owned by the firm. The two major _____ classes are tangible _____s and intangible _____s.
   a. Income
   b. Asset
   c. EBITDA
   d. Accounts payable

8. In finance, the _____ of a financial asset measures the sensitivity of the asset's price to interest rate movements, expressed as a number of years. The reason for expressing this sensitivity in years is that the time that will elapse until a cash flow is received allows more interest to accumulate. Therefore the price of an asset with long term cashflows has more interest rate sensitivity than an asset with cashflows in the near future.
   a. Macaulay duration
   b. 4-4-5 Calendar
   c. Yield to maturity
   d. Duration

9. The _____ is a financial and accounting term for the difference between the duration of assets and liabilities, and is typically used by banks, pension funds, or other financial institutions to measure their risk due to changes in the interest rate. This is one of the mismatches that can occur and are known as asset liability mismatches. Another way to define _____ is : it is the difference in the sensitivity of interest-yielding assets and the sensitivity of liabilities (of the organization) to a change in market interest rates (yields.)
   a. Modern portfolio theory
   b. Debt cash flow
   c. Net worth
   d. Duration gap

10. _____ means the inability to pay one's debts as they fall due. Usually used in Business terms, _____ refers to the inability for a 'limited liability' company to pay off debts.

This is defined in two different ways:

Cash flow _____ -
    Unable to pay debts as they fall due.
Balance sheet _____ -
    Having negative net assets: liabilities exceed assets; or net liabilities.

   a. Interest
   b. Insolvency
   c. AAB
   d. A Random Walk Down Wall Street

11. In accounting, _____ or *Carrying value* is the value of an asset according to its balance sheet account balance. For assets, the value is based on the original cost of the asset less any depreciation, amortization or impairment costs made against the asset. A company's _____ is its total assets minus intangible assets and liabilities.
   a. Current liabilities
   b. Pro forma
   c. Retained earnings
   d. Book value

12. _____ or fair value accounting refers to the accounting standards of assigning a value to a position held in a financial instrument based on the current fair market price for the instrument or similar instruments. Fair value accounting has been a part of US Generally Accepted Accounting Principles (GAAP) since the early 1990s. The use of fair value measurements has increased steadily over the past decade, primarily in response to investor demand for relevant and timely financial statements that will aid in making better informed decisions.
   a. 529 plan
   b. 4-4-5 Calendar
   c. Mark-to-market
   d. 7-Eleven

13. _____ is the price at which an asset would trade in a competitive Walrasian auction setting. _____ is often used interchangeably with open _____, fair value or fair _____, although these terms have distinct definitions in different standards, and may differ in some circumstances.

Chapter 22. Managing Interest Rate Risk and Insolvency Risk on the Balance Sheet

International Valuation Standards defines _____ as 'the estimated amount for which a property should exchange on the date of valuation between a willing buyer and a willing seller in an arm'e;s-length transaction after proper marketing wherein the parties had each acted knowledgeably, prudently, and without compulsion.'

_____ is a concept distinct from market price, which is 'e;the price at which one can transact'e;, while _____ is 'e;the true underlying value'e; according to theoretical standards.

   a. Wrap account
   b. Market value
   c. Debt restructuring
   d. T-Model

14. In business, _____ is the total assets minus total outside liabilities of an individual or a company. For a company, this is called shareholders' equity and may be referred to as book value. _____ is stated as at a particular point in time.
   a. Restructuring
   b. Moneylender
   c. Certified International Investment Analyst
   d. Net worth

15. The _____ is a United States government corporation created by the Glass-Steagall Act of 1933. It provides deposit insurance, which guarantees the safety of checking and savings deposits in member banks, currently up to $250,000 per depositor per bank. Insured deposits are backed by the full faith and credit of the United States.
   a. NYSE Group
   b. Federal Deposit Insurance Corporation
   c. Ford Foundation
   d. FASB

16. The _____ is a financial ratio used to compare a company's book value to its current market price. Book value is an accounting term denoting the portion of the company held by the shareholders; in other words, the company's total tangible assets less its total liabilities. The calculation can be performed in two ways, but the result should be the same each way. In the first way, the company's market capitalization can be divided by the company's total book value from its balance sheet. The second way, using per-share values, is to divide the company's current share price by the book value per share (i.e. its book value divided by the number of outstanding shares).
   a. Price-to-book ratio
   b. Whisper numbers
   c. Stop order
   d. Stock repurchase

Chapter 23. Managing Risk with Derivative Securities

1. In finance, a _____ is a standardized contract, to buy or sell a specified commodity of standardized quality at a certain date in the future, at a market determined price (the futures price.)

The price is determined by the instantaneous equilibrium between the forces of supply and demand among competing buy and sell orders on the exchange at the time of the purchase or sale of the contract.

In many cases, the items may be such non-traditional 'commodities' as foreign currencies, commercial or government paper [e.g., bonds], or 'baskets' of corporate equity ['stock indices'] or other financial instruments.

- a. Futures contract
- b. Heston model
- c. Financial future
- d. Repurchase agreement

2. _____ is the discipline of identifying, monitoring and limiting risks. In some cases the acceptable risk may be near zero. Risks can come from accidents, natural causes and disasters as well as deliberate attacks from an adversary.
- a. 4-4-5 Calendar
- b. Penny stock
- c. FIFO
- d. Risk management

3. _____ is a structured finance process that involves pooling and repackaging of cash-flow-producing financial assets into securities, which are then sold to investors. The term '_____' is derived from the fact that the form of financial instruments used to obtain funds from the investors are securities. As a portfolio risk backed by amortizing cash flows - and unlike general corporate debt - the credit quality of securitized debt is non-stationary due to changes in volatility that are time- and structure-dependent.
- a. Special journals
- b. Reputational risk
- c. The Glass-Steagall Act of 1933
- d. Securitization

4. In financial accounting, a _____ or statement of financial position is a summary of a person's or organization's balances. Assets, liabilities and ownership equity are listed as of a specific date, such as the end of its financial year. A _____ is often described as a snapshot of a company's financial condition.
- a. Statement on Auditing Standards No. 70: Service Organizations
- b. Balance sheet
- c. Financial statements
- d. Statement of retained earnings

5. _____ is the provision of resources (such as granting a loan) by one party to another party where that second party does not reimburse the first party immediately, thereby generating a debt, and instead arranges either to repay or return those resources (or material(s) of equal value) at a later date. The first party is called a creditor, also known as a lender, while the second party is called a debtor, also known as a borrower.

Movements of financial capital are normally dependent on either _____ or equity transfers.

- a. Warrant
- b. Credit
- c. Clearing house
- d. Comparable

6. _____ is the risk of loss due to a debtor's non-payment of a loan or other line of credit (either the principal or interest (coupon) or both)

Chapter 23. Managing Risk with Derivative Securities

Most lenders employ their own models (credit scorecards) to rank potential and existing customers according to risk, and then apply appropriate strategies. With products such as unsecured personal loans or mortgages, lenders charge a higher price for higher risk customers and vice versa. With revolving products such as credit cards and overdrafts, risk is controlled through careful setting of credit limits.

a. Liquidity risk
b. Transaction risk
c. Credit risk
d. Market risk

7. A _____ is a financial contract whose value is derived from the value of something else (known as the underlying.) The underlying on which a _____ is based can be an asset, weather conditions bonds or other forms of credit.
a. Derivative
b. 7-Eleven
c. 529 plan
d. 4-4-5 Calendar

8. A _____ is a fungible, negotiable instrument representing financial value. They are broadly categorized into debt securities (such as banknotes, bonds and debentures), and equity securities; e.g., common stocks. The company or other entity issuing the _____ is called the issuer.
a. Security
b. Book entry
c. Securities lending
d. Tracking stock

9. A _____ is an agreement between two parties to buy or sell an asset at a specified point of time in the future. The price of the underlying instrument, in whatever form, is paid before control of the instrument changes. This is one of the many forms of buy/sell orders where the time of trade is not the time where the securities themselves are exchanged.
a. Constant maturity credit default swap
b. Loan Credit Default Swap Index
c. Derivatives markets
d. Forward contract

10. A _____ is an exchange of promises between two or more parties to do an act which is enforceable in a court of law. It is where an unqualified offer meets a qualified acceptance and the parties reach Consensus ad Idem. The parties must have the necessary capacity to _____ and the _____ must not be either trifling, indeterminate, impossible or illegal.
a. 529 plan
b. 4-4-5 Calendar
c. 7-Eleven
d. Contract

11. A _____ is a foreign exchange agreement between two parties to exchange principal and fixed rate interest payments on a loan in one currency for principal and fixed rate interest payments on an equal (regarding net present value) loan in another currency. They are motivated by comparative advantage.
a. Foreign exchange market
b. Currency swap
c. Forex swap
d. Currency pair

12. In finance, a _____ is a position established in one market in an attempt to offset exposure to the price risk of an equal but opposite obligation or position in another market -- usually, but not always, in the context of one's commercial activity. Hedging is a strategy designed to minimize exposure to such business risks as a sharp contraction in demand for one's inventory, while still allowing the business to profit from producing and maintaining that inventory. A typical hedger might be a farmer with 2000 acres of unharvested wheat in the ground, who would rather tend his crop without the distraction of uncertain prices.

Chapter 23. Managing Risk with Derivative Securities

a. Hedge
b. 7-Eleven
c. 4-4-5 Calendar
d. 529 plan

13. In finance, a _____ is a derivative in which two counterparties agree to exchange one stream of cash flows against another stream. These streams are called the legs of the _____.

The cash flows are calculated over a notional principal amount, which is usually not exchanged between counterparties.

a. Volatility swap
b. Swap
c. Volatility arbitrage
d. Local volatility

14. _____ in finance is the risk associated with imperfect hedging using futures. It could arise because of the difference between the asset whose price is to be hedged and the asset underlying the derivative, or because of a mismatch between the expiration date of the futures and the actual selling date of the asset.

Under these conditions, the spot price of the asset, and the futures price, do not converge on the expiration date of the future.

a. Liquidity risk
b. Currency risk
c. Credit risk
d. Basis risk

15. In finance, a _____ is a debt security, in which the authorized issuer owes the holders a debt and, depending on the terms of the _____, is obliged to pay interest (the coupon) and/or to repay the principal at a later date, termed maturity.

Thus a _____ is a loan: the issuer is the borrower, the _____ holder is the lender, and the coupon is the interest. _____s provide the borrower with external funds to finance long-term investments, or, in the case of government _____s, to finance current expenditure.

a. Puttable bond
b. Catastrophe bonds
c. Bond
d. Convertible bond

16. The _____ is a financial market where participants buy and sell debt securities, usually in the form of bonds. As of 2006, the size of the international _____ is an estimated $45 trillion, of which the size of the outstanding U.S. _____ debt was $25.2 trillion.

Nearly all of the $923 billion average daily trading volume in the U.S. _____ takes place between broker-dealers and large institutions in a decentralized, over-the-counter market.

a. 529 plan
b. 4-4-5 Calendar
c. Fixed income
d. Bond market

17. A _____ is a listing of bonds or fixed income instruments and a statistic reflecting the composite value of its components. It is used as a tool to represent the characteristics of its component fixed income instruments. They differ from stock market indices in their complexity.

a. 7-Eleven
b. 4-4-5 Calendar
c. Bond market index
d. 529 plan

18. _____ is a fee paid on borrowed assets. It is the price paid for the use of borrowed money , or, money earned by deposited funds . Assets that are sometimes lent with _____ include money, shares, consumer goods through hire purchase, major assets such as aircraft, and even entire factories in finance lease arrangements.
   a. Interest
   b. AAB
   c. Insolvency
   d. A Random Walk Down Wall Street

19. An _____ is the price a borrower pays for the use of money they do not own, and the return a lender receives for deferring the use of funds, by lending it to the borrower. _____s are normally expressed as a percentage rate over the period of one year.

_____s targets are also a vital tool of monetary policy and are used to control variables like investment, inflation, and unemployment.

   a. ABN Amro
   b. A Random Walk Down Wall Street
   c. AAB
   d. Interest rate

20. An _____ is a contract written by a seller that conveys to the buyer the right -- but not the obligation -- to buy (in the case of a call _____) or to sell (in the case of a put _____) a particular asset, such as a piece of property such as, among others, a futures contract. In return for granting the _____, the seller collects a payment (the premium) from the buyer.

For example, buying a call _____ provides the right to buy a specified quantity of a security at a set strike price at some time on or before expiration, while buying a put _____ provides the right to sell.

   a. Option
   b. AT'T Mobility LLC
   c. Amortization
   d. Annuity

21. A _____ is a financial contract between two parties, the buyer and the seller of this type of option. Often it is simply labeled a 'call'. The buyer of the option has the right, but not the obligation to buy an agreed quantity of a particular commodity or financial instrument (the underlying instrument) from the seller of the option at a certain time (the expiration date) for a certain price (the strike price.)
   a. Bear spread
   b. Call option
   c. Bear call spread
   d. Bull spread

22. A _____ is a financial contract between two parties, the seller (writer) and the buyer of the option. The put allows its buyer the right but not the obligation to sell a commodity or financial instrument (the underlying instrument) to the writer (seller) of the option at a certain time for a certain price (the strike price.) The writer (seller) has the obligation to purchase the underlying asset at that strike price, if the buyer exercises the option.
   a. Bear call spread
   b. Debit spread
   c. Bear spread
   d. Put option

Chapter 23. Managing Risk with Derivative Securities

23. An _____ is a derivative in which one party exchanges a stream of interest payments for another party's stream of cash flows. _____s can be used by hedgers to manage their fixed or floating assets and liabilities. They can also be used by speculators to replicate unfunded bond exposures to profit from changes in interest rates.

    a. Interest rate swap
    b. Equity swap
    c. Implied volatility
    d. International Swaps and Derivatives Association

24. In general, _____ means to allow a positive value and a negative value to set-off and partially or entirely cancel each other out.

In the context of credit risk, there are at least three specific types of _____:

- Close-out _____

- _____ by novation

- Settlement or payment _____

_____ decreases credit exposure, increases business with existing counterparties, and reduces both operational and settlement risk and operational costs.

    a. Reinvestment risk
    b. Moneylender
    c. Netting
    d. Forward price

25. In the original and simplified sense, _____ were things of value, of uniform quality, that were produced in large quantities by many different producers; the items from each different producer are considered equivalent. It is the contract and this underlying standard that define the commodity, not any quality inherent in the product.

_____ exchanges include:

- Chicago Board of Trade
- Kansas City Board of Trade
- Euronext.liffe
- Kuala Lumpur Futures Exchange
- Bhatinda Om ' Oil Exchange
- London Metal Exchange
- New York Mercantile Exchange
- Multi Commodity Exchange
- Dalian Commodity Exchange

Markets for trading _____ can be very efficient, particularly if the division into pools matches demand segments. These markets will quickly respond to changes in supply and demand to find an equilibrium price and quantity.

a. Commodities
c. 529 plan
b. 7-Eleven
d. 4-4-5 Calendar

26. The U.S. _____ is an independent agency of the United States government which holds primary responsibility for enforcing the federal securities laws and regulating the securities industry, the nation's stock and options exchanges, and other electronic securities markets. The SEC was created by section 4 of the SEC of 1934 (now codified as 15 U.S.C. Â§ 78d and commonly referred to as the 1934 Act.)

a. 7-Eleven
c. Securities and Exchange Commission
b. 4-4-5 Calendar
d. 529 plan

Chapter 24. Managing Risk With Loan Sales and Securitization

1. A _____ is a firm that quotes both a buy and a sell price in a financial instrument or commodity, hoping to make a profit on the bid/offer spread, or turn.

In foreign exchange trading, where most deals are conducted over-the-counter and are, therefore, completely virtual, the _____ sells to and buys from its clients. Hence, the client's loss and the spread is the _____ firm's profit, which gets thus compensated for the effort of providing liquidity in a competitive market.

   a. 529 plan
   b. 7-Eleven
   c. 4-4-5 Calendar
   d. Market maker

2. A _____ (or 'syndicated bank facility') is a large loan in which a group of banks provide funds for a borrower, usually several but without joint liability. There is usually a lead bank or group of banks (the 'Arranger/s' or 'Agent/s') that takes a percentage of the loan and syndicates or sells the rest to other banks. In contrast, a bilateral loan, only involves one borrower and one lender (often a bank or financial institution.)
   a. Debt buyer
   b. Credit score
   c. Collection agency
   d. Syndicated loan

3. In financial accounting, a _____ or statement of financial position is a summary of a person's or organization's balances. Assets, liabilities and ownership equity are listed as of a specific date, such as the end of its financial year. A _____ is often described as a snapshot of a company's financial condition.
   a. Statement on Auditing Standards No. 70: Service Organizations
   b. Financial statements
   c. Balance sheet
   d. Statement of retained earnings

4. _____ is a measure of the ability of a debtor to pay their debts as and when they fall due. It is usually expressed as a ratio or a percentage of current liabilities.

For a corporation with a published balance sheet there are various ratios used to calculate a measure of liquidity.

   a. Operating leverage
   b. Invested capital
   c. Accounting liquidity
   d. Operating profit margin

5. _____ arises from situations in which a party interested in trading an asset cannot do it because nobody in the market wants to trade that asset. _____ becomes particularly important to parties who are about to hold or currently hold an asset, since it affects their ability to trade.

Manifestation of _____ is very different from a drop of price to zero.

   a. Currency risk
   b. Liquidity risk
   c. Tracking error
   d. Credit risk

6. In finance, 'participation' is an ownership interest in a mortgage or other loan. In particular, _____ is a cooperation of multiple lenders to issue a loan (known as participation loan) to one borrower. This is usually done in order to reduce individual risks of the lenders.
   a. Doctrine of the Proper Law
   b. Short positions
   c. Securitization
   d. Loan participation

Chapter 24. Managing Risk With Loan Sales and Securitization

7. In economics, the concept of the _____ refers to the decision-making time frame of a firm in which at least one factor of production is fixed. Costs which are fixed in the _____ have no impact on a firms decisions. For example a firm can raise output by increasing the amount of labour through overtime.

   a. Long-run
   b. 529 plan
   c. Short-run
   d. 4-4-5 Calendar

8. _____ is a term in Corporate Finance used to indicate a condition when promises to creditors of a company are broken or honored with difficulty. Sometimes _____ can lead to bankruptcy. _____ is usually associated with some costs to the company and these are known as Costs of _____.

   a. Cashflow matching
   b. Capital structure
   c. Commercial paper
   d. Financial distress

9. A _____ or bank is a financial institution whose primary activity is to act as a payment agent for customers and to borrow and lend money.

   The first modern bank was founded in Italy in Genoa in 1406, its name was Banco di San Giorgio (Bank of St. George.)

   Many other financial activities were added over time.

   a. 4-4-5 Calendar
   b. Banker
   c. Black Sea Trade and Development Bank
   d. Bought deal

10. A _____ is a professionally managed type of collective investment scheme that pools money from many investors and invests it in stocks, bonds, short-term money market instruments, and/or other securities. The _____ will have a fund manager that trades the pooled money on a regular basis. Currently, the worldwide value of all _____s totals more than $26 trillion.

    Since 1940, there have been three basic types of investment companies in the United States: open-end funds, also known in the US as _____s; unit investment trusts (UITs); and closed-end funds.

    a. Financial intermediary
    b. Mutual fund
    c. Net asset value
    d. Trust company

11. _____ are dollar-denominated bonds, issued mostly by Latin American countries in the 1980s, named after U.S. Treasury Secretary Nicholas Brady.

    _____ were created in March 1989 in order to convert bonds issued by mostly Latin American countries into a variety or 'menu' of new bonds after many of those countries defaulted on their debt in the 1980's. At that time, the market for sovereign debt was small and illiquid, and the standardization of emerging-market debt facilitated risk-spreading and trading.

    a. Coupon rate
    b. Brady bonds
    c. Nominal yield
    d. Municipal bond

Chapter 24. Managing Risk With Loan Sales and Securitization

12. In finance, a _____ is a debt security, in which the authorized issuer owes the holders a debt and, depending on the terms of the _____, is obliged to pay interest (the coupon) and/or to repay the principal at a later date, termed maturity.

Thus a _____ is a loan: the issuer is the borrower, the _____ holder is the lender, and the coupon is the interest. _____s provide the borrower with external funds to finance long-term investments, or, in the case of government _____s, to finance current expenditure.

a. Puttable bond
b. Catastrophe bonds
c. Bond
d. Convertible bond

13. _____ is that which is owed; usually referencing assets owed, but the term can cover other obligations. In the case of assets, _____ is a means of using future purchasing power in the present before a summation has been earned. Some companies and corporations use _____ as a part of their overall corporate finance strategy.

a. Debt
b. Credit cycle
c. Partial Payment
d. Cross-collateralization

14. _____ is the corporate management term for the act of reorganizing the legal, ownership, operational, or other structures of a company for the purpose of making it more profitable or better organized for its present needs. Alternate reasons for restructing include a change of ownership or ownership structure, demerger repositioning debt _____ and financial _____.

a. Restructuring
b. Day trading
c. Cross-border leasing
d. Concentrated stock

15. In finance, a _____ is a derivative in which two counterparties agree to exchange one stream of cash flows against another stream. These streams are called the legs of the _____.

The cash flows are calculated over a notional principal amount, which is usually not exchanged between counterparties.

a. Volatility swap
b. Local volatility
c. Swap
d. Volatility arbitrage

16. _____ is a structured finance process that involves pooling and repackaging of cash-flow-producing financial assets into securities, which are then sold to investors. The term '_____' is derived from the fact that the form of financial instruments used to obtain funds from the investors are securities. As a portfolio risk backed by amortizing cash flows - and unlike general corporate debt - the credit quality of securitized debt is non-stationary due to changes in volatility that are time- and structure-dependent.

a. The Glass-Steagall Act of 1933
b. Reputational risk
c. Securitization
d. Special journals

17. A _____ is a fungible, negotiable instrument representing financial value. They are broadly categorized into debt securities (such as banknotes, bonds and debentures), and equity securities; e.g., common stocks. The company or other entity issuing the _____ is called the issuer.

Chapter 24. Managing Risk With Loan Sales and Securitization

a. Security
b. Book entry
c. Securities lending
d. Tracking stock

18. The _____ is a U.S. government-owned corporation within the Department of Housing and Urban Development

Ginnie Mae provides guarantees on mortgage-backed securities backed by federally insured or guaranteed loans, mainly loans issued by the Federal Housing Administration, Department of Veterans Affairs, Rural Housing Service, and Office of Public and Indian Housing. Ginnie Mae securities are the only MBS that are guaranteed by the United States government.

a. Certified Emission Reductions
b. Cash budget
c. Case-Shiller Home Price Indices
d. GNMA

19. _____ is the process of decreasing an amount over a period of time. The word comes from Middle English amortisen to kill, alienate in mortmain, from Anglo-French amorteser, alteration of amortir, from Vulgar Latin admortire to kill, from Latin ad- + mort-, mors death. Particular instances of the term include:

- _____ (business), the allocation of a lump sum amount to different time periods, particularly for loans and other forms of finance, including related interest or other finance charges.
    - _____ schedule, a table detailing each periodic payment on a loan (typically a mortgage), as generated by an _____ calculator.
    - Negative _____, an _____ schedule where the loan amount actually increases through not paying the full interest
- Amortized analysis, analyzing the execution cost of algorithms over a sequence of operations.
- _____ of capital expenditures of certain assets under accounting rules, particularly intangible assets, in a manner analogous to depreciation.
- _____ (tax law)

_____ is also used in the context of zoning regulations and describes the time in which a property owner has to relocate when the property's use constitutes a preexisting nonconforming use under zoning regulations.

- Depreciation

a. Amortization
b. AT'T Inc.
c. Intrinsic value
d. Option

20. _____ is early repayment of a loan by a borrower.

In the case of a mortgage-backed security (MBS), _____ is perceived as a risk, because mortgage debts are often paid off early in order to incur lower total interest payments through cheaper refinancing. The new financing may be cheaper because the borrower's credit rating has improved or because interest rates are lower, but in either case, the payments that would have been made to the MBS investor would be above market rates.

Chapter 24. Managing Risk With Loan Sales and Securitization

a. Bankruptcy remote
b. Disposal tax effect
c. Prepayment
d. Retention ratio

21. _____s (_____s) are a form of securitization where payments from multiple middle sized and large business loans are pooled together and passed on to different classes of owners in various tranches.

Each class of owner may receive larger payments in exchange for being the first in line to lose money if the businesses fail to repay the loans. The actual loans used are generally multi-million dollar loans known as syndicated loans, usually originally lent by a bank with the intention of the loans being immediately paid off by the _____ owners.

a. Tick size
b. Fiscal sponsorship
c. Financial rand
d. Collateralized loan obligation

22. A _____ is a financial debt vehicle that was first created in June 1983 by investment banks Salomon Brothers and First Boston for Freddie Mac. (The First Boston team was led by Dexter Senft.) Legally, a _____ is a special purpose entity that is wholly separate from the institution(s) that create it.

a. Yield curve spread
b. Collateralized mortgage obligation
c. 4-4-5 Calendar
d. Tranche

23. _____ is a fee paid on borrowed assets. It is the price paid for the use of borrowed money, or, money earned by deposited funds. Assets that are sometimes lent with _____ include money, shares, consumer goods through hire purchase, major assets such as aircraft, and even entire factories in finance lease arrangements.

a. AAB
b. A Random Walk Down Wall Street
c. Insolvency
d. Interest

24. In business and accounting, _____s are everything of value that is owned by a person or company. The balance sheet of a firm records the monetary value of the _____s owned by the firm. The two major _____ classes are tangible _____s and intangible _____s.

a. Accounts payable
b. Income
c. EBITDA
d. Asset

25. _____ is a term that refers both to:

- a formal discipline used to help appraise, or assess, the case for a project or proposal, which itself is a process known as project appraisal; and
- an informal approach to making decisions of any kind.

Under both definitions the process involves, whether explicitly or implicitly, weighing the total expected costs against the total expected benefits of one or more actions in order to choose the best or most profitable option.

A hallmark of _____ is that all benefits and all costs are expressed in money terms, and are adjusted for the time value of money, so that all flows of benefits and flows of project costs over time (which tend to occur at different points in time) are expressed on a common basis in terms of their present value.

a. Cost-benefit analysis
c. 4-4-5 Calendar
b. 7-Eleven
d. 529 plan

26. _____ is one of the authors of the Black-Scholes equation. In 1997 he was awarded the Nobel Memorial Prize in Economic Sciences for 'a new method to determine the value of derivatives'. The model provides the fundamental conceptual framework for valuing options, such as calls or puts, and is referred to as the Black-Scholes model, which has become the standard in financial markets globally.

a. Adolph Coors
c. Andrew Tobias
b. Robert James Shiller
d. Myron Samuel Scholes

ANSWER KEY

Chapter 1
1. d	2. a	3. d	4. b	5. d	6. c	7. a	8. a	9. a	10. d
11. c	12. a	13. b	14. c	15. d	16. b	17. c	18. a	19. d	20. d
21. d	22. c	23. c	24. a	25. c	26. c				

Chapter 2
1. c	2. d	3. b	4. d	5. b	6. a	7. d	8. d	9. a	10. d
11. a	12. d	13. c	14. a	15. c	16. d	17. d	18. d	19. d	20. d
21. a	22. d	23. d	24. b	25. d	26. a	27. c	28. a	29. c	30. a
31. d	32. c	33. a	34. d	35. d	36. d				

Chapter 3
1. c	2. d	3. d	4. d	5. a	6. d	7. d	8. d	9. d	10. d
11. d	12. a	13. a	14. b	15. a	16. d	17. d	18. d	19. c	20. d

Chapter 4
1. d	2. d	3. d	4. d	5. a	6. d	7. d	8. d	9. a	10. d
11. d	12. a	13. d	14. d	15. c	16. d	17. d	18. a	19. d	20. b
21. c									

Chapter 5
1. d	2. c	3. c	4. d	5. b	6. d	7. c	8. d	9. b	10. d
11. d	12. d	13. a	14. d	15. c	16. a	17. d	18. b	19. d	20. a
21. d	22. b	23. b	24. d	25. c	26. d	27. d	28. c		

Chapter 6
1. d	2. a	3. c	4. d	5. d	6. c	7. d	8. d	9. a	10. c
11. c	12. c	13. d	14. a	15. d	16. a	17. a	18. c	19. d	20. d
21. d	22. d	23. d	24. d	25. a	26. d	27. d	28. d	29. d	30. d
31. a	32. d	33. d	34. a	35. d	36. a	37. a	38. d	39. c	40. d
41. d	42. d	43. d	44. a	45. a	46. b	47. b			

Chapter 7
1. c	2. d	3. d	4. d	5. c	6. d	7. d	8. d	9. a	10. d
11. b	12. d	13. d	14. d	15. a	16. d	17. d	18. b	19. d	20. d
21. b	22. d	23. d	24. a	25. d	26. d	27. a	28. a	29. c	30. d
31. d	32. d	33. d	34. d	35. a	36. d	37. d	38. d	39. d	40. d
41. d									

Chapter 8
1. d	2. b	3. b	4. b	5. d	6. d	7. d	8. d	9. b	10. b
11. c	12. a	13. a	14. c	15. d	16. b	17. a	18. d	19. d	20. b
21. d	22. d	23. b	24. d	25. a	26. c	27. d	28. d	29. d	30. c
31. d	32. d	33. d	34. b						

Chapter 9

1. d	2. d	3. b	4. d	5. d	6. b	7. a	8. d	9. d	10. d
11. d	12. b	13. d	14. b	15. d	16. d	17. d	18. d	19. d	20. d
21. d	22. c	23. d	24. d	25. d	26. a	27. d	28. d	29. d	30. d
31. c	32. a	33. a	34. d	35. d	36. d	37. b	38. a	39. d	40. c
41. c	42. a	43. d	44. a	45. c	46. c	47. d	48. c	49. d	50. b
51. a	52. b	53. c	54. d						

Chapter 10

1. d	2. d	3. c	4. d	5. d	6. a	7. d	8. d	9. b	10. b
11. d	12. c	13. a	14. d	15. c	16. a	17. d	18. d	19. d	20. d
21. b	22. d	23. d	24. b	25. d	26. c	27. d	28. a	29. d	30. b
31. a	32. d	33. d	34. a	35. d	36. d	37. b	38. a	39. d	40. d
41. d	42. d	43. b	44. c	45. d	46. d	47. d	48. c	49. d	

Chapter 11

1. d	2. a	3. a	4. b	5. d	6. d	7. d	8. c	9. c	10. b
11. d	12. a	13. a	14. d	15. d	16. c	17. b	18. d	19. d	20. a
21. d	22. d	23. a	24. d	25. d	26. d	27. c	28. d	29. d	30. a
31. d	32. d								

Chapter 12

1. d	2. d	3. d	4. d	5. d	6. d	7. d	8. d	9. d	10. d
11. d	12. a	13. d	14. b	15. d	16. d	17. d	18. d	19. a	20. c
21. d	22. b	23. c	24. d	25. d	26. a	27. c	28. a	29. b	30. a
31. d	32. d	33. a	34. d						

Chapter 13

1. d	2. d	3. b	4. a	5. b	6. d	7. d	8. d	9. a	10. c
11. b	12. d	13. b	14. c	15. d	16. d	17. a	18. d	19. d	20. d
21. c									

Chapter 14

1. c	2. d	3. d	4. a	5. a	6. a	7. c	8. c	9. c	10. d
11. d	12. b	13. d	14. b	15. b	16. d	17. d	18. d	19. b	20. d

Chapter 15

1. b	2. b	3. b	4. a	5. d	6. c	7. c	8. b	9. c	10. d
11. c	12. d	13. a	14. d	15. d	16. d				

Chapter 16

1. c	2. a	3. d	4. b	5. a	6. b	7. c	8. d	9. c	10. d
11. a	12. c	13. c	14. d	15. d	16. a	17. b	18. d	19. d	20. a

ANSWER KEY

Chapter 17
1. d   2. c   3. a   4. d   5. d   6. b   7. d   8. d   9. d   10. d
11. c   12. d   13. d   14. a   15. d   16. d   17. d   18. c   19. b   20. d
21. d   22. a   23. d   24. c   25. b   26. a   27. b   28. d   29. d   30. c

Chapter 18
1. d   2. d   3. a   4. c   5. d   6. b   7. d   8. d   9. d   10. d
11. d   12. a   13. d   14. d   15. d

Chapter 19
1. c   2. b   3. d   4. d   5. d   6. b   7. d   8. d   9. a   10. a
11. b   12. d   13. b   14. c   15. d   16. d   17. b   18. a   19. a   20. d
21. b   22. d   23. b   24. d   25. d   26. a

Chapter 20
1. d   2. a   3. d   4. c   5. d   6. d   7. d   8. d   9. d   10. d
11. c   12. b   13. b   14. d   15. d   16. a   17. d   18. d   19. b   20. c
21. d   22. d   23. b   24. c   25. d   26. d   27. d   28. d   29. a   30. d
31. c   32. d   33. d   34. d   35. c   36. b   37. d   38. d   39. a   40. d
41. d   42. d   43. d   44. b   45. d   46. b   47. a   48. b

Chapter 21
1. d   2. c   3. d   4. a   5. b   6. d   7. d   8. d   9. b   10. a
11. d   12. a   13. d   14. c   15. d   16. d   17. d   18. b   19. d

Chapter 22
1. d   2. d   3. a   4. d   5. d   6. a   7. b   8. d   9. d   10. b
11. d   12. c   13. b   14. d   15. b   16. a

Chapter 23
1. a   2. d   3. d   4. b   5. b   6. c   7. a   8. a   9. d   10. d
11. b   12. a   13. b   14. d   15. c   16. d   17. c   18. a   19. d   20. a
21. b   22. d   23. a   24. c   25. a   26. c

Chapter 24
1. d   2. d   3. c   4. c   5. b   6. d   7. c   8. d   9. b   10. b
11. b   12. c   13. a   14. a   15. c   16. c   17. a   18. d   19. a   20. c
21. d   22. b   23. d   24. d   25. a   26. d

www.ingramcontent.com/pod-product-compliance
Lightning Source LLC
Chambersburg PA
CBHW082040230426
43670CB00016B/2723